Is Your Lesson for You or Your Students?

Connecting with students on a personal level is a very important aspect of teaching, but how can we ensure students are just as connected to what they're learning? *Is Your Lesson for You or Your Students?* answers this question by providing a student-centered, culturally responsive, and curriculum-aligned framework that teachers can easily implement into their classrooms.

Author Jahkari "JT" Taylor, a seasoned educational leader and instructional coach, walks readers through his I.C.E.D. T.E.A. acronym to enrich the instructional capacity of K–12 educators. Each chapter contains professional insight, research-based approaches, reflection questions, and practical strategies for leveraging knowledge of students to inspire learning in the academic setting. Downloadable resources, such as the I.C.E.D. T.E.A. Framework, the Checklist for Aligning Curriculum, and the PACE Framework, are also provided to cultivate reflective practitioners and help teachers prioritize their students and methodology.

Whether you're a veteran educator or just starting your teaching career, you'll come away with a plethora of strategies for creating student-centered lessons, maximizing student achievement, and creating enjoyable learning experiences for all students.

Jahkari H. Taylor is an experienced, award-winning educational leader, researcher, and school improvement consultant for K–12 school divisions and universities across the United States. He was included in Inside Business's Top Forty Under Forty in Hampton Roads, VA in 2021 and was named an ASCD Emerging Leader in 2019. He currently coaches principals and teachers regarding culturally responsive teaching practices, social-emotional learning, specially designed instruction, reframing discipline, and instructional excellence.

Also Available from Routledge Eye On Education
(www.routledge.com/k-12)

The Student Motivation Handbook: 50 Ways to Boost an Intrinsic Desire to Learn
Larry Ferlazzo

Passionate Learners, Second Edition: How to Engage and Empower Your Students
Pernille Ripp

What Great Teachers Do Differently, Third Edition: 19 Things That Matter Most
Todd Whitaker

Tangible Equity: A Guide for Leveraging Student Identity, Culture, and Power to Unlock Excellence In and Beyond the Classroom
Colin Seale

Identity Affirming Classrooms: Spaces that Center Humanity
Erica Buchanan-Rivera

Culturally Responsive Education in the Classroom: An Equity Framework for Pedagogy
Adeyemi Stembridge

Is Your Lesson for You or Your Students?

A Framework for Student-Centered, Culturally Responsive, and Aligned Instruction

Jahkari H. Taylor

NEW YORK AND LONDON

Designed cover image: Getty Images

First published 2025
by Routledge
605 Third Avenue, New York, NY 10158

and by Routledge
4 Park Square, Milton Park, Abingdon, Oxon, OX14 4RN

Routledge is an imprint of the Taylor & Francis Group, an informa business

© 2025 Jahkari H. Taylor

The right of Jahkari H. Taylor to be identified as author of this work has been asserted in accordance with sections 77 and 78 of the Copyright, Designs and Patents Act 1988.

All rights reserved. No part of this book may be reprinted or reproduced or utilised in any form or by any electronic, mechanical, or other means, now known or hereafter invented, including photocopying and recording, or in any information storage or retrieval system, without permission in writing from the publishers.

Trademark notice: Product or corporate names may be trademarks or registered trademarks, and are used only for identification and explanation without intent to infringe.

ISBN: 978-1-041-01196-5 (hbk)
ISBN: 978-1-041-01214-6 (pbk)
ISBN: 978-1-003-61362-6 (ebk)

DOI: 10.4324/9781003613626

Typeset in Palatino
by KnowledgeWorks Global Ltd.

Dedication

This book is dedicated to all of the educators who show up for children each day with a sense of purpose and conviction. I also dedicate this book to my wife who serves as an elementary school principal, my mother who is a retired educator, and my children who have always been my inspiration to do what is best for all children.

Contents

Acknowledgments viii
Meet the Author ix
Poem: Who's Got the T.E.A.? x
Poem: ICED TEA in the Classroom xi
Preface: Who's Got the Tea?: Student-Centered, Culturally
  Responsive, and Aligned Instruction xii
Introduction: What Type of "T.E.A." Do Students Prefer? xv

Section 1: Who Do I Teach? 1

1 The "I" in I.C.E.D. T.E.A.: Identity 3

2 The "C" in I.C.E.D. T.E.A.: Culture 11

3 The "E" in I.C.E.D. T.E.A.: Empowerment 30

4 The "D" in I.C.E.D. T.E.A.: Dreams 41

Section 2: How Do I Teach? 51

5 The "T" in I.C.E.D. T.E.A.: Transformative Rapport 53

6 The "E" in I.C.E.D. T.E.A.: Engaging Instruction 66

7 The "A" in I.C.E.D. T.E.A.: Aligned Curriculum 78

  Conclusion: Fill Your Cup First 96

  Appendix A: The I.C.E.D. T.E.A. Framework 100
  Appendix B: Checklist for Aligning the Curriculum 102
  Appendix C: CIA Alignment Practice Tool (APT) 105
  Appendix D: The Purpose Pedagogical Approach 106

Acknowledgments

I would like to thank every educational researcher and practitioner who has come before me. I am fully aware that I am standing on the shoulders of giants who have sacrificed so much to improve educational outcomes for students.

I would also like to thank Lauren Davis for her commitment to editing my manuscript and to all those who supported this endeavor.

Lastly, I must thank God for His presence and power in my life. I am aware of the divine assignment that has been given to me to play a pivotal role in the transformation of communities. I am fully committed to my purpose.

Meet the Author

Dr. Jahkari "JT" Taylor is an award-winning educator, researcher, published author, and full-time educational consultant. He currently serves as the President and CEO of Purpose Pushers LLC, where he partners with non-profit organizations, K–12 schools, colleges, and universities nationwide to deliver dynamic professional learning opportunities.

Dr. Taylor partners with school leaders and teachers in three key areas: 1) Organizational Leadership, 2) Instructional Leadership, and 3) Professional Development Planning. He is committed to building individual capacity while inspiring organizational success. Dr. Taylor is on a mission to play a pivotal role in the transformation of communities.

He has over 17 years of experience as an executive coach, educational consultant, Title 1 instructional coach, and special education teacher. He has presented at the national conferences of many professional organizations and has been featured in a WHRO commercial titled "The Teaching Profession."

Dr. Taylor was the Iota Phi Lambda Emerald Educator, Teacher of the Year at Oscar F. Smith High School, Overall City-Wide Teacher of the Year for Chesapeake Public Schools, and 2019 ASCD Emerging Leader. In 2021, Dr. Taylor was selected as one of Inside Business's Top 40 Under 40 in the Hampton Roads region of Virginia for exemplifying success in business and commitment to community service.

He has four earned degrees, including two master's and a Doctor of Philosophy in Advanced Educational Leadership from Regent University.

His motto is simple: "Know Your Why!"

Poem: Who's Got the T.E.A.?

"T" represents "Transformative Rapport"
The ability to connect with students when they walk through the door

Leveraging relationships to improve the score
"No significant learning occurs without significant relationships," Dr. James Comer told us before

"E" represents "Engaging Instruction"
I'm talking neural impulses firing off like a volcanic eruption

Every student at attention, no heads on the desk
Prepared to unleash brilliance because life is a test

"A" is for alignment
Understand your assignment
Don't teach for compliance
But speak to the giant

On the inside of every child
Tremendous potential behind every smile

Who's Got the T.E.A.?

Poem: ICED TEA in the Classroom

Imagine a long journey in the blistering heat
Feeling beat, like a fight with Muhammed Ali
Sweat dripping from your face and flooding the street
That's when you need something cold and refreshingly sweet
ICED Tea to the rescue, now have a seat

Relax your mind, as I pour your cup
We got sugar, honey, iced tea all mixed up

It's the perfect blend of relaxation
A few ice cubes, and I'm on vacation

Can you see the waves, can you feel the breeze
It's the experience of joy that we all need

Especially in schools, kids want the same thing
A place to be free, emotional safety
Every student wants to say, "The school embraced me"
When I needed to be refreshed, they poured ICED TEA

ICED TEA in the Classroom

Preface: Who's Got the Tea?

Student-Centered, Culturally Responsive, and Aligned Instruction

Academic achievement for students in the United States has been steadily declining over the past few years. This decline has been reported by the National Assessment of Educational Progress (NAEP), also known as The Nation's Report Card, which measures the educational achievement and progress of students across the United States. According to NAEP, students have struggled in both math and reading, but math scores have revealed the largest declines since NAEP began tracking long-term trends in student achievement (Schwartz, 2023). The report clearly highlights that the methods being used in classrooms across the country are not working for all students. I argue that the educational system needs to return to the basics of teaching and learning by simplifying the focus to quality relationships and quality instruction.

This book offers a student-centered, culturally responsive, and aligned instructional framework that prioritizes quality relationships and quality instruction. This approach to increasing student achievement is rooted in two guiding questions: 1) who do you teach, and 2) how should you teach them? The metaphor and acronym for I.C.E.D T.E.A. is employed to explain what I consider the best instructional methodology for engaging diverse students in the teaching and learning process. I have chosen to metaphorically encourage educators to make "iced tea" in the classroom because of its significance to me personally. It's nostalgic for me. It reminds me of pastimes and experiences that stir feelings of childlike innocence, independence, joy, and freedom. In addition, I use the acronym for I.C.E.D. T.E.A. because it will serve as an unforgettable mnemonic device to help educators understand the need to perfectly blend culturally responsive instructional methods to meet the unique needs of diverse learners.

As a beverage, iced tea comprises several elements that, when isolated, can effectively stand on their own. No question water, the contents within a tea bag, lemon, and sugar can exist as individual items, but when you blend them, something magical, desirable, and refreshing is born. I believe educators can create a similar experience for students in the learning environment. If there was ever a time when students were thirsty for something magical, desirable, and refreshing in schools, it is now. Therefore, I argue that every teacher in the K–12 setting must figuratively make iced tea by employing a blended methodology that combines a student-centered, culturally responsive, and aligned instructional approach.

Structure of the Book

This book is divided into two sections. Each section is guided by a question to help prompt reflection and introspection prior to reading. Additionally, each chapter concludes with reflective questions and a chapter summary. Section 1 is titled "Who Do I Teach?" and Section 2 is titled "How Do I Teach?" These two guiding questions are designed to help educators keep students at the forefront of their consciousness at all times. Chapters 1–4 are found in Section 1, and Chapters 5–7 are in Section 2.

In Chapter 1, we explore the "I" of the I.C.E.D. T.E.A. Framework, which represents *Identity*. This chapter highlights the importance of centering student identity in the classroom and discusses the role of student identity as it relates to the relationship-building process. In Chapter 2, we explore "C," which refers to *Culture*. In this chapter, readers will learn the importance of prioritizing students' culture and employing culturally responsive teaching practices to maximize student achievement.

Chapter 3, which begins with "E," explores the concept of *Empowerment*. This chapter sheds light on why teachers must consider student efficacy as they learn the empowerment needs of their students. This chapter aims to inspire teachers to empower students as independent learners. Chapter 4 concludes Section 1. This chapter begins with "D" and emphasizes the need to leverage students' *Dreams* to foster personal and academic connections in the learning environment.

Section 2 moves readers from "Who Do I Teach?" to "How Do I Teach?" This section shifts from learning about students to learning how to teach them based on their individual identities, cultures, empowerment needs, and dreams. Continuing with our acronym for I.C.E.D. T.E.A., Chapter 5 begins with "T," which stands for *Transformative rapport*. This section is about the supremacy of relationships in the school context and the need to apply a relational teaching methodology to drive academic achievement.

Chapter 6 begins with "E" and focuses on *Engaging instruction*. In this chapter, readers will explore research and strategies for engaging students from behavioral, emotional, and cognitive dimensions. In Chapter 7 we focus on the letter "A," which refers to *Aligned curriculum*. This chapter informs educators of the pitfalls of failing to align curriculum, instruction, and assessments. In the concluding chapter, we bring it all together by emphasizing what can happen when I.C.E.D. T.E.A. is intentionally brought into the educational system to improve the performance of diverse learners.

Reference

Schwartz, S. (2023, June 21). Reading and math achievement is getting worse, nation's report card shows. *EducationWeek*. https://www.edweek.org/leadership/reading-and-math-achievement-is-getting-worse-nations-report-card-shows/2023/06

Introduction: What Type of "T.E.A." Do Students Prefer?

In 2014, I was asked to sit on an expert panel with several experienced educators. The panel's goal was to provide new beginning teachers with practical "nuggets of wisdom" to help them begin their journey in education. The event organizers within our school district specifically asked the panelists to help new teachers understand what being a teacher is all about. They insisted that we stay away from the deep theoretical underpinnings of pedagogy to avoid overwhelming those entering the field of education with no experience. I vividly remember the excitement, passion, and joy exuding from the new teachers, many of whom had just graduated from teacher preparation programs across the nation. While they bombarded the panel with a host of thought-provoking questions, I noticed that the overall theme of their questions pertained to the subject matter they were eager to teach. Some asked about the utility of Shakespearean literature in a secondary English class, some asked about the appropriateness of calculators in an elementary setting, and others were concerned about how much time they would need to allocate toward developing lesson plans.

While I believed their questions were appropriate and legitimate, I also felt that most of the questions leaned heavily toward a "teacher-centered" approach to education. A teacher-centered approach to education is a pedagogical approach where the teacher's voice, interests, and needs take precedence over the students' voices, interests, and needs. According to Dr. Joseph Lathan of the University of San Diego, a teacher-centered approach is "the more traditional or conventional approach to teaching" (2024, p. 1). This approach has many pros, especially when delivering direct and explicit instruction. So, I am not advocating for abolishing teacher-centered approaches entirely.

> A teacher-centered approach to education is a pedagogical approach where the teacher's voice, interests, and needs take precedence over the students' voices, interests, and needs.

However, I am advocating for a blended approach that moves students from the margins and toward the center.

That day, I sat on the panel expecting at least one person to say, "What is it like working with 20 to 30 young people for eight hours a day?" I expected someone to ask, "What's the secret for maintaining students' attention?" Yet, none of those questions popped up. So, when it was my turn to address the collective group, I stood up and said, "All of your questions have been great, but one question that you might want to think about is *'who you will be teaching*?'" I explained, "It is likely that you will encounter some students who will not be as passionate about the subject matter you teach as you are. Nevertheless, you will still be responsible for engaging those students. This will require you to develop a connection with the students first, to help them connect with the content you teach." After I finished making my points, most of the expert panelists nodded in agreement, and some applauded. I intentionally tried to shift the conversation to a more student-centered focus.

At that time in my professional career, I had been a classroom educator for only five years. I did not consider myself an instructional leader, but I did consider myself effective at building relationships with students and centering learning around their interests and needs. I was a special educator tasked with implementing individualized education plans (IEPs) to increase the academic achievement and functional performance of students identified as having an emotional disability. Working in the inclusion setting and writing IEPs forced me to develop an instructional mindset rooted in personalizing student learning. This is the teaching methodology I seek to offer in this book. I am advocating for a pedagogical approach described as student-centered, culturally responsive, and aligned to the curriculum.

"Are My Lessons for Me or My Students?"

One of the most important questions I want educators to reflect on throughout this book is, "Are my lessons for me or my students?" This question is designed to help educators be mindful of who is at the center of their educational philosophy and pedagogy. Additionally, it is a question that challenges educators' methodology; more specifically, how they design and deliver instruction. To spur reflection, an educator must look no further than their classroom. What motivated you to decorate your classroom the way that you did? Why did you design and deliver your most recent lesson the way that you did? When you constructed that lesson, did you consider which students might respond with disengagement?

When you create activities, projects, and other assessments, who serves as the motivation for your actions? Let me put it this way: Are you keeping your students at the center of your work? If one of your students were to ask if you were designing lessons based on their interests, needs, and lived experiences, what would you say? Could you prove that you intentionally create learning opportunities based on your students' interests, needs, and lived experiences? Could you prove your lessons are student-centered, culturally responsive, and aligned to the curriculum?

These reflective questions are important if an educator desires to create engaging and enjoyable learning experiences for all students. However, if teachers are content with the traditional approach of centering the personal interests, needs, and lived experiences of adults, they risk student engagement and, ultimately, student success. This is obviously not the purpose and goal of teaching. As educators, we should not strive to create lessons that we enjoy. We should aim to create lessons that students enjoy. For that reason, I ask every educator to answer this question: "Are your lessons for you or your students?"

When students sense that a lesson is irrelevant to their interests and realities, they often respond with apathy. Some students withdraw from the learning environment or begin to engage in horseplay when they sense that a lesson is boring. I have learned that some students will disconnect and detach from the teaching and learning process to communicate non-verbal feedback to educators. Instead of rudely expressing, "This lesson sucks," some students gently place their heads on the desk to communicate their disinterest in the lesson plan design and delivery. One way to prevent student apathy and detachment from the learning environment is to practice a pedagogy rooted in what students consider enjoyable and interesting.

Yet, to accomplish this task, teachers must develop an adequate understanding of the students they teach. This can only be achieved if educators actively and continuously seek to learn their students' interests, needs, lived experiences, and preferences. I always say, "The greatest instructional tool a teacher can have is knowledge about their students." If you know what gives your students a sense of happiness and purpose, you can devise activities around it. If you know what brings your students joy, you can integrate that into the lesson design and delivery. I believe teachers can significantly increase student engagement if they successfully create lessons based on what their students adore.

The Power of Preference

Every child has desires rooted in their unique preferences. In other words, they want what they want. As a young man who grew up in the southeastern region of Virginia, I developed an affinity for teas of all kinds. My mother introduced me to tea at an early age. She would keep a stash of Lipton lemon tea or peppermint tea in the cabinet. While she would make her hot tea with a spoonful of honey, I preferred my tea iced with plenty of sugar. I am talking about the type of tea normally found in your local convenience store that is premixed with an unnecessarily high sugar content. While I am certain that I was in love with tea that could probably induce a diabetic coma, that was my preference. I did not necessarily dislike my mother's tea, but it was just not "my cup of tea."

Since my youthful cravings were always more powerful than my ability to abstain and control my sweet tooth, it was not uncommon for me to beg my mother for a dollar so I could walk to the candy lady's house to buy a cold Brisk tea, a bag of chips, and 25 cents' worth of candy. For those unfamiliar with the concept of a "candy lady," please allow me to explain. A "candy lady" is an individual who functions like a convenience store within a community. Instead of going to a 7-Eleven or another convenience store for snacks, a kid in my community could easily walk to the candy lady who sold Snickers, Mr. Goodbars, pickles, cookies, drinks, and other popular snacks from the comfort of her house. The candy lady played a major role in my upbringing as I did not have my own transportation to frequent local convenience stores. So, when I wanted a snack and my preferred drink of choice, a sweet tea, I would walk a few short minutes to the candy lady. No matter how hot it was during those summer mornings in Virginia, I knew I would be refreshed once I got my hands on an ice-cold sweet tea.

Lived Experiences and Academic Connections

As I reflect on my childhood, I realize that going to the Candy Lady during elementary school was much more than a casual stroll to satisfy my youthful cravings. I mean, it was an opportunity to appease my sweet tooth, but at the same time, it was also much more than that. For me, every trip to the candy lady was empowering. It offered me an opportunity to act independently. It allowed me to employ self-determination and self-advocacy skills because I had to express to an adult what I desired for myself. In addition, it allowed me to employ academic skills in a practical manner. I had to add my coins, subtract the cost of what I wanted to purchase, and effectively pay the candy lady. I had to strategize and engage in cost comparison to ensure I received a good deal. To some degree, a trip to the candy lady illustrates a powerful example of what schooling can be for young people. One trip epitomized academic rigor. It provided me with a practical learning experience that required the application of a variety of academic skills, and it was centered around my interests and preferences as a young person. We must try our best to replicate this type of experience for students in schools today.

Leveraging Students' Lived Experiences and Interests

Prior to becoming a full-time education consultant, I was a special educator and Title 1 Instructional Coach. I served in these roles for 12 years in the K–12 setting, and it was that experience that taught me that the best way to engage young people in the teaching and learning process was to make sure their interests, needs, and desires were prioritized in the academic setting. I learned to focus my energy and efforts on designing lessons my students preferred to engage in. For example, if students were interested in hip-hop,

I would incorporate the elements of hip-hop to promote literacy instruction. If the students were interested in sports, I would integrate sports into our daily lessons to teach mathematical concepts. Likewise, if students were interested in specific clothing brands, I would integrate popularized fashion trends into my lessons to present academic content in a creative way.

I encourage educators in today's classrooms to use the same approach. If students in today's classrooms spend the majority of their time at home playing Roblox and Fortnite or watching TikTok and YouTube, it would be prudent for educators to increase the use of these elements in the learning environment. The goal should be to leverage students' interests to maximum learning in the classroom. This is the student-centered approach to teaching and learning that I am advocating for in this book.

Designing Lessons With Students in Mind

Every educator must understand that students' lived experiences represent valuable resources that can be integrated into the learning environment to increase student engagement and achievement. For example, as a student, I would have been more inclined to write journal entries or short narratives about my trips to the candy lady than to engage in random assignments based on my teachers' interests. I would have leapt at the opportunity to participate in math assignments that required me to use Skittles as manipulatives to cultivate my number sense and mathematical computation skills, as opposed to counting oranges or apples on a boring worksheet downloaded from the internet. Although I despised word problems, I may have been more inclined to engage in word problems that used language and concepts that I was familiar with. Here are a few examples of word problems that could have integrated elements from my childhood:

- If Jim's mother gave him 2 dollars and 50 cents, how many cans of iced tea could he purchase if the cans cost 50 cents each at the candy lady?
- How much money would Jim need if Jim desired to purchase a Chico Stick for 25 cents and a pack of Boston Baked Beans for 15 cents?

These examples are rooted in what I preferred during my elementary school years: candy – meaning, I may have been more inclined to engage in academic assignments simply based on the fact that they would have been related to my lived experiences and preferences. Educators must understand that every child is an expert in their own lived experiences. Therefore, teachers must try to tap into students' expertise and integrate it into the learning environment to bridge the gap from the students' world to the academic world.

I believe there is an entire generation of students in today's schools who are eagerly waiting for an opportunity to engage in lessons that are rooted in their realities and preferences. I am sure students who enjoy playing Roblox would be more likely to engage in writing assignments that require them to describe games that they have created while playing Roblox. I believe students who enjoy playing Fortnite would be more inclined to engage in word problems that incorporate elements from Fortnite. Unfortunately, some students will never get the opportunity to engage in lessons specifically designed for them. This is because far too many educators are clinging to an archaic method of teacher-centered instruction that fails to center students' interests, needs, and preferences. Undoubtedly, this must change.

A Blended Instructional Approach Is Warranted

Considering what I now know about so-called "achievement gaps," culturally responsive approaches, and the unique characteristics of students from today's generation, I promote a blended instructional approach rooted in a student-centered, culturally responsive, and aligned teaching methodology. The question educators must ask themselves is simple: Is it an achievement gap or a gap in student-centered, culturally responsive, and aligned instruction? My 17 years of experience working in the K–12 setting has led me to believe that achievement gaps are the consequence of instruction that fails to reach specific populations. I believe these students who typically are on the "short end of the instructional stick" are motivated and inspired by their own interests, experiences, and preferences. Therefore, teachers must consider whether they are designing lessons for themselves or their students. If you are still figuratively serving the type of tea that my mother enjoyed, do not feel ashamed. It was perfect for my mother's generation. However, today's generation may appreciate iced tea. All we have to do is change our approach instead of forcing students to accept what they do not enjoy. Let's make I.C.E.D. T.E.A. on purpose!

Reference

Lathan, J. (2024). *Complete guide to student-centered vs. teacher-centered learning. University of San Diego Online.* https://onlinedegrees.sandiego.edu/teacher-centered-vs-student-centered-learning

Section 1

Who Do I Teach?

Guiding Question #1: Who Do I Teach?

Tea is a popular beverage that is enjoyed worldwide. If we plan on serving tea to our guests, it would be most beneficial to know how the people we intend on serving like their tea. Some people prefer a traditional cup with sliced lemon, some like the base to be half water and half lemonade (also known as a Sunjoy at Chick-fil-A), and others prefer it to be customized based on their unique cultural ways and lived experiences. In some cases, people like it without any sweetener at all. Nevertheless, the moral of the story is everyone has a preference. As the teacher serving as the resident "tea mixologist" in the classroom setting, you are responsible for preparing the type of "tea" your students consider most appetizing to their unique taste buds and preferences.

The guiding question for this section must always remain at the forefront of everything educators do. This question is, "Who do I teach?" This question compels educators to prioritize getting to know their students on a personal level. Educators can accomplish this by exploring four concepts that will allow them to comprehensively understand who they intend to engage in the teaching and learning process. These concepts can be best understood through the acronym *I.C.E.D.*, which stands for *Identity, Culture, Empowerment,* and *Dreams*.

1

The "I" in I.C.E.D. T.E.A.
Identity

Establishing quality relationships with students is necessary to maximize student academic achievement. To start this process, teachers must commit to developing a deeper understanding of their students by first seeking to understand their students' identities. As you read this chapter, I encourage you to visualize and reimagine a learning environment committed to valuing and honoring students' identities. Imagine a place designed to nurture a genuine sense of self-love and security among students. Imagine a space where every child feels affirmed and validated for who they are, not just based on their performance. Visualize a place where every child feels as if they belong. Your classroom and your school must become that place for every child.

What Is Identity?

Who do you think you are? Who do your students think they are? These questions speak to the matter of identity. In the most general sense, identity refers to a person's sense of self. So, your identity is how you perceive yourself and what you think others perceive about you. The same is true

> Identity is how you perceive yourself and what you think others perceive about you.

DOI: 10.4324/9781003613626-2

for students. How students view themselves and what they think others believe about them can be construed as their identity. A person's identity begins to be formed as soon as they enter this world, and this profoundly impacts how one chooses to live and behave. While identity may seem static, it is much more nuanced than we think. According to Walker (2022), "For decades, scholars in organizational and social psychology have distinguished between two types of identity: personal and social" (p. 73). Walker argues that personal and social identities are not distinct from each other but somewhat different aspects of the same thing. In other words, how a person perceives themselves and how they are perceived in society is all a matter of identity.

According to Stanford Center for Teaching and Learning (n.d.), "Everyone has many identities. Age, gender, religious or spiritual affiliation, sexual orientation, race, ethnicity, and socioeconomic status are all identities." Some identities are easily identifiable (i.e., race), while others may not be visible (i.e., socioeconomic status). Nevertheless, identities are constructed within a social context. This means "the broader society, over history, has defined, ascribed meaning, and given status and power to various identities" (Stanford Center for Teaching and Learning, n.d.). Due to how students are socialized by their identity within the broader society, they may feel empowered, disempowered, accepted, or rejected in the school context. This can present numerous issues for students. For this reason, educators need to understand how social identities impact student learning and behavioral performance in the classroom.

In an article titled "Navigating Social Identity in the Classroom," the author Jackson Bartlett (2022) states, "Social identities can shape students' learning experiences positively or negatively" (p. 1). For example, a student with a disability may be socialized in school by their disability. This means when a student with a disability interacts with other students with disabilities in a classroom setting, they may feel a sense of acceptance or belonging because of shared traits and characteristics. Yet, when the same student interacts with their non-disabled peers, that sense of acceptance and belonging may be compromised. This same concept can be applied along the lines of racial identity, cultural identity, gender identity, and so on. Therefore, teachers must develop an understanding of their students' identities to intentionally create an inclusive environment where each child feels a sense of acceptance and belonging. Several researchers (Allen et al., 2018; Gopalan & Brady, 2019; Hurtado et al., 2007) have found that a sense of belonging is positively associated with student engagement, persistence, mental health, prosocial behaviors, and overall academic performance. By centering students' identities and proactively creating an atmosphere within the learning context where each child feels accepted for who they are, teachers ultimately provide students with the best opportunity to thrive in school.

The Nuance of Identity and the Relationship-Building Process

Understanding the complex and nuanced identities of the students entering classrooms today is challenging for most educators. Still, educators must attempt to understand students on a personal level. I do not believe an educator can effectively engage students while ignoring their identities. Therefore, understanding student identities is one prerequisite for employing a student-centered and culturally responsive approach to teaching and learning. Additionally, understanding student identity is necessary to effectively engage students in the relationship-building process.

Dr. James Comer, Professor of Child Psychiatry at Yale University, said, "No significant learning occurs without a significant relationship." Every effective educator knows this to be true. My question is, how can teachers build effective relationships with students while dismissing their identities? How can teachers connect with students they refuse to get to know or understand? I believe this would be an impossible task because getting to know a person is the first step to building a relationship with that person. Hence, seeking to understand students' identities is inherent in the relationship-building process.

Throughout my 17 years working in K–12 schools, I have learned that every effective educator uses relationships to drive student achievement. Relationships are the vehicle that transports students from disengagement and mediocrity to engagement and excellence. Every time I speak with effective educators, they confirm that their secret to maximizing student learning and achievement involves building relationships with students. I have also learned that not every educator knows how to effectively build relationships with students, especially culturally diverse students. Many do not know where to begin the relationship-building process. I believe understanding student identity is the first step.

Strategies for Leveraging Student Identity to Build Relationships

Getting to know students is the starting point for building effective relationships with them, and building relationships with students is the secret to maximizing their achievement. Countless researchers and practitioners corroborate this belief: when educators prioritize building relationships with students, they are more likely to draw students into the learning process.

> When educators prioritize building relationships with students, they are more likely to draw students into the learning process.

In a 2019 article titled "Why Teacher-Student Relationships Matter: New Findings Shed Light on Best Approaches," Sarah Sparks explained that "A review of educational research analysis of 46 studies found that strong teacher-student relationships were associated in both the short- and long-term with improvements on practically every measure schools care about: higher student academic engagement, attendance, grades, fewer disruptive behaviors and suspensions, and lower school dropout rates." Sparks also stated, "Those effects were strong even after controlling for differences in students' individual, family, and school backgrounds." Sparks (2019) highlights the fact that building relationships with students can lead to positive outcomes for every student regardless of identity differences.

While each student benefits from the relationship-building process, no blanket strategy will work to build a relationship with each student. Students are not a monolith. Therefore, teachers must seek to gain as much information as possible about each student. This is why understanding student identity is imperative. Teachers can get to know students on an individual level by employing a variety of student-interest surveys. A **student**

interest survey is a tool that allows teachers to gather data on students' interests, needs, and preferences (Brenna et al., 2017). Student interest surveys can help educators learn what makes students "tick."

Additionally, they can help to amplify students' voices by allowing them to communicate directly with teachers. Teachers do not have to try to guess or make assumptions about what students are interested in or need; they can allow students to express their interests and needs directly through student interest surveys. Although a quick Google search can provide educators with thousands of student interest surveys, I encourage educators to consider using their creativity to make customized student surveys that are grade-level specific. By administering student surveys, educators can gain meaningful information that helps them better understand their students.

Another strategy that can help educators learn about student identity is to conduct brief **interviews** with students or their families. Like student interest surveys, interviews can provide educators with information about students' identities while also building a sense of trust. I always encourage educators to have their interview questions previewed by their colleagues to ensure the questions are age-appropriate, culturally sensitive, and respectful. If educators are not careful, they can ask questions that are too intrusive or harmful. When interviewing students, the goal is always to ensure psychological safety. Educators can use Google Forms to create student interest surveys or interview questions. By using Google Forms, educators can retrieve and store data that is easily accessible during the lesson planning process. Integrating information gained directly from students into the lesson planning process or learning environment has the greatest likelihood of increasing engagement because it is relevant to student's interests and needs as communicated by students and their families.

Reflective Questions for Chapter 1

Who are my students? How do they identify racially, ethnically, and culturally? Are they self-proclaimed gamers or sports fanatics? Do they identify with people from affluent communities in suburbia? Do they identify with people who live in communities characterized by skyscraper apartment buildings in large, densely populated urban cities? Do they identify with people from rural communities? Do my students enjoy spending time on TikTok, Instagram, or YouTube? Are they enamored with Roblox, Fortnite, or a sports-related video game? What do they do for fun while at home? Do my students have access to the internet and technology at home? Do my students identify with military families who are regularly expected to relocate? Do they live with one parent, two parents, grandparents, or foster parents? Would my students describe themselves as introverted, extroverted, or "will talk when trust is established"?

These questions can help educators better understand who they are responsible for teaching. In addition, these questions can serve as a guide to measure how much educators know about the students they are trying to teach. Once information about students' identities is gained, educators can easily use it to plan lessons or deliver instruction. Again, if our aim is to design student-centered instruction, we must develop a comprehensive understanding of who our students are.

Review of Summarized Findings from This Chapter:

1. Commit to learning about the role of social identities in the classroom.
2. Prioritize the relationship-building process.
3. Make a concerted effort toward understanding student identities.
4. Employ multiple strategies, such as the following:
   a. Use student and parent questionnaires.
   b. Utilize student interest surveys.
   c. Interview students and guardians.
      i. Phone interviews.
      ii. Virtual interviews (i.e., Zoom, Google Hangouts, Microsoft Teams, etc.).
         - Virtual interviews can be a helpful strategy that removes transportation barriers, ultimately providing a more convenient option for guardians.
5. Amplify student voice by employing "Get to Know You" activities and journal prompts that allow students to share details about themselves.

References

Allen, K-A., Kern, M., Vella-Brodrick, D., Hattie, J., & Waters, L. (2018). What schools need to know about fostering school belonging: A meta-analysis. *Educational Psychology Review, 30*, 1–34.

Bartlett, J. (2022, August 8). *Navigating social identity in the classroom*. University of Illinois Chicago Center for the Advancement of Teaching Excellence.

Brenna, B. et al. (2017). Exploring the use of interest inventories with elementary students: A rich foundation for literacy curriculum making. *The Reading Professor, 39*(1), 6–12. https://scholar.stjohns.edu/thereadingprofessor/vol39/iss1/6?utm_source=scholar.stjohns.edu%2Fthereadingprofessor%2Fvol39%2Fiss1%2F6&utm_medium=PDF&utm_campaign=PDFCoverPages

Gopalan, M., & Brady, S. T. (2019). College students' sense of belonging: A national perspective. *Educational Researcher, 49*(2), 134–137. https://doi.org/10.3102/0013189X19897622

Hurtado, S., Han, J. C., Sáenz, V. B., Espinosa, L. L., Cabrera, N. L., & Cerna, O. S. (2007). Predicting transition and adjustment to college: Biomedical and behavioral science aspirants' and minority students' first year of college. *Research in Higher Education, 48*(7), 841–887. https://doi.org/10.1007/s11162-007-9051-x

Sparks, S. (2014, November 26). Emotionally disturbed students at greatest risk of dropping out, study finds. *EducationWeek*. https://www.edweek.org/teaching-learning/emotionally-disturbed-students-at-greatest-risk-of-dropping-out-study-finds/2014/11

Sparks, S. (2019, March 12). Why teacher-student relationships matter. *EducationWeek*. https://www.edweek.org/teaching-learning/why-teacher-student-relationships-matter/2019/03

Stanford Center for Teaching and Learning. (n.d.). Student identities. https://ctl.stanford.edu/student-identities

Walker, B. W. (2022). A dynamic reframing of the social/personal identity dichotomy. *Organizational Psychology Review, 12*(1), 73–104. https://doi.org/10.1177/20413866211020495

2

The "C" in I.C.E.D. T.E.A.
Culture

The new census data released in 2020 indicates that the United States has more racially and ethnically diverse groups today than at any other point in our nation's history (Coritz et al., 2023). This means that educators today are responsible for teaching the most culturally diverse student population in US history. Thus, educators must understand culture and how it impacts student learning. Culture is often generally defined as how people live, but in the context of schools it is much more than that. Culture influences the way students process information, interact with others, and respond to adversity. Culture also influences how students dress, the type of music they listen to, and the vocabulary they use to communicate. Culture is a significant part of students' identities, and it impacts every detail of student life. Yet, culture is difficult to define because of its inherent complexities and diverse expressions. Nevertheless, educators must strive to center students' culture in the academic space.

What Is Culture?

A simple Google search will prove that countless different definitions of "culture" exist in our world. Causadias (2020) explains, "Culture is a fuzzy concept without fixed boundaries, meaning different things according to situations" (p. 310). What makes defining culture even more complicated is the fact that different disciplines seem to define it based on the perspective of individuals within that particular discipline. For example, biologists, ethnographers, and sociologists may all study the concept of culture. They may all attempt to define culture in a way that is useful for others studying culture within their field or discipline. The issue is that not everyone will agree with each other's definitions. So, what is my recommendation based on this complicated situation of defining culture? While this may add to the confusion revolving around the definition of "culture," I believe the field of education must also grapple with a definition of culture that is appropriate and helpful for individuals within the field of education.

Culture … in the Field of Education

As mentioned earlier, culture is "fuzzy" and difficult to define. Yet, I believe any and every attempt by educators to understand students' culture ultimately places educators in a more advantageous position than ignoring or abandoning the concept. So, here are a few definitions that I think can be helpful for educators seeking to understand culture:

1. Neuroscientist Antonio Damasio suggests that "culture is a regulator of human life and identity" (Jandt, 2004, p. 5).
2. American anthropologist Ruth Benedict explains that culture is "what binds men together … the ideas and standards they have in common" (Samovar et al., 2012, p. 10).
3. Educator and author Zaretta Hammond believes that culture "is the way that every brain makes sense of the world … it is the software for the brain's hardware" (Hammond, 2015, p. 22).
4. Samovar et al. (2012) state, "Culture is the rules for living and functioning in society … it is the rules for playing the game of life" (p. 11).
5. According to the Encyclopedia Britannica, "culture includes language, ideas, beliefs, customs, codes, institutions, tools, techniques, works of art, rituals, and ceremonies, among other elements" (White, 2022).

> Culture is the inspiration and chief influence behind all human activity. It influences how individuals live, behave, and represent themselves. It also influences how individuals perceive ideas and process information to make sense of the world around them.

Based on the five references above, it is easy to understand why one concrete, agreed-upon definition of culture is difficult to find. Nevertheless, I submit that culture is the inspiration and chief influence behind all human activity. It influences how individuals live, behave, and represent themselves. It also influences how individuals perceive ideas and process information to make sense of the world around them. From an academic standpoint, culture significantly impacts how students interact with and perceive the learning environment. Therefore, it plays a significant role in the teaching and learning process.

Culture plays a role in providing students and educators with their self-concept. It influences how students and educators interact within the educational setting, and it dictates attitudes, beliefs, preferences, and interests. As Zaretta Hammond eloquently articulated, "Culture is the way that every brain makes sense of the world." Due to its impact on cognition, culture is inseparable from the teaching and learning process. For this reason, educators must strive to understand the cultures with which their students identify as well as the cultures with which they identify as educators. Prioritizing culture within the school setting will help to reduce the negative consequences associated with two major barriers to student achievement: cultural mismatch and deficit thinking.

Cultural Mismatch

Cultural mismatch and deficit thinking are believed to hinder the academic and behavioral outcomes of diverse students (Chu, 2016; Dudley-Marling, 2015; Keefer, 2017; Irvine, 2012). According to Fuller (2021), "Cultural mismatch is defined by difference in race, ethnicity, or culture between the teacher and student" (p. 3). McGrady and Reynolds (2013) assert that cultural mismatch has the potential to adversely impact students of color. They wrote, "Unfortunately, substantial scholarly evidence indicates that teachers – especially White teachers – evaluate Black students' behavior and academic potential more negatively than those of white students" (p. 3). The negative outcomes associated with cultural mismatch were also observed among Latinx students and other students of color (Kozlowski, 2015; Recknagel et al., 2022; Valenzuela, 1999). This dilemma is often attributed to subconsciously held racial stereotypes, biases, and misunderstandings of the cultural differences between teachers and students.

Cultural mismatch and cultural misunderstandings are believed to contribute to a host of negative outcomes for students, including all the following: "miscommunication; confrontations; hostility; alienation; diminished self-esteem; and possible misclassification in special education programs" (Irvine, 2009). Since 80% of the teacher workforce in the United States identifies as white, and over 50% of the nation's student population identifies as students of color, educators must develop an approach to teaching and learning that combats the negative outcomes associated with cultural mismatch (U.S. Department of Education, 2016).

Deficit Thinking

In addition to cultural mismatch, another significant barrier to student success is deficit thinking. In an article titled "The Miseducation of a Beginning Teacher: One Educator's Critical Reflections on the Functions and Power of Deficit Narratives," Terry Pollack (2012) shares her experiences working as a new beginning teacher in a diverse urban school. As a curious new beginning teacher, Pollack explained that she often inquired about achievement disparities between racially diverse students. She noted that "explanations were conveyed through compelling stories told by experienced, caring, and well-intentioned classroom teachers, principals, and support staff" (p. 94). On one occasion, a cooperating teacher told Pollack to let a particular student, Darnell, sleep in class. The cooperating teacher explained that Darnell should be able to sleep in class because school was "the only place he could get any sleep." The cooperating teacher further explained that Darnell lived with his "welfare-dependent mother" in a chaotic home. In some way, the narrative provided about Darnell's home life justified why any effort to engage him in the teaching and learning process was considered a waste of time. Pollack highlighted that the teacher ended the conversation by stating, "Darnell is lost to us. He'll probably never see his 18th birthday."

Pollack (2012) explained that this cooperative teacher had a reputation for being "motherly," "generous," and "caring." Yet, this teacher perpetuated a deficit narrative about students of color. Pollack noted that deficit thinking can be revealed through casual "teacher talk" that takes place in workrooms, professional learning communities, and department meetings. In some cases, educators reinforce deficit narratives about racial/cultural "others" without realizing the miseducation they are providing to everyone who absorbs the conversations (p. 93). Deficit narratives can cause educators to embrace lowered expectations for students that ultimately lead to less access to rigorous learning opportunities.

Patton Davis and Museus (2019) state, "Deficit thinking holds students from historically oppressed populations responsible for the challenges and inequalities they face" (p. 119). Opposed to considering the myriad factors (educator capacity, historical inequities, systematic issues, etc.) that may contribute to the lack of academic achievement for minoritized students, deficit thinking "situates school failure in the minds, bodies, communities, and culture of students" (Dudley-Marling, 2015, p. 1). Typically, deficit thinking and cultural mismatch will be sustained in schools where student culture is disregarded, undermined, or viewed as "the big bad boogeyman" that must never be discussed.

I argue that every teacher in every school must commit to learning about students' cultural backgrounds through an asset-based lens as opposed to a deficit lens. If educators are not intentional about viewing students' cultural backgrounds from an asset-based perspective, they are likely to view them from a deficit-based lens. Educators who embrace and perpetuate deficit paradigms place minoritized students in a disadvantaged position. Therefore, deficit thinking must be challenged.

A Research-Based Solution: Culturally Responsive Teaching

Prioritizing culture within the school context and effectively applying the practices associated with culturally responsive teaching can help to counter the negative impact of cultural mismatch and deficit thinking. According to Dr. Geneva Gay (2018), culturally responsive teaching refers to "using the cultural knowledge, prior experiences, frames of reference, and performance styles of ethnically diverse students to make learning encounters more relevant to and effective for them" (p. 36). In other words, educators must gain cultural knowledge and insight about the students they teach, and then integrate that information into the teaching and learning process. This approach should be applied to every aspect of the school. This means that the classroom, the lesson plan design, the curricular materials, and the manner in which instruction is delivered should be designed with students in mind. Culturally responsive teaching centers the students and their cultural backgrounds in the learning environment.

To effectively engage students with this approach, teachers must possess knowledge about the students' lived experiences, current realities, and preferences. The more educators know about students' culture, prior experiences, preferences, aspirations, etc., the better equipped educators will be to respond appropriately to meet the unique needs of each student. According to Abacioglu et al. (2020), culturally responsive teaching has been "found to be related to positive student outcomes, such as increased student engagement, better achievement, and more positive peer relationships" (p. 737). Therefore, educators must first center students' culture in the academic setting, and then employ practices associated with culturally responsive teaching if they want to improve student outcomes.

Three Culturally Responsive Strategies

For educators who desire to remove the ideology of deficit thinking from the school's culture, I encourage you to cultivate empathy, culturally responsive teaching self-efficacy (CRTSE), and Collective Culturally Responsive Efficacy (CCRE). This is a sequential process that must begin in the hearts and minds of educators. From one educator to a grade-level or department of teachers, and finally from a group, it should culminate as a movement within the school building as a whole. By engaging theories around empathy, self-efficacy, and collective teacher efficacy, educators will inevitably begin the self-reflective process of recalibrating attitudes, beliefs, and dispositions pertaining to meeting the unique needs of students from culturally diverse backgrounds.

Strategy #1 – Empathy: An Essential Teaching Disposition
One scholar who has masterfully studied the relationship between empathy and culturally responsive teaching is Dr. Chezare Warren, an Associate Professor of Equity and Inclusion in Education Policy at Vanderbilt University's Peabody College of Education and Human Development. In an article titled "Towards a Pedagogy for the Application of Empathy in Culturally Diverse Classrooms," Warren (2013) explores the relevance of empathy in the teaching profession as a disposition of teachers aiming to enact culturally responsive teaching practices. He found that when applied as a teaching disposition, empathy can lead to improved academic outcomes for culturally diverse students, and Black males in particular.

After reviewing historical literature related to empathy in education and other fields, Warren (2013) described empathy as "how the teacher (observer) responded to and interacted with students (target)" (p. 397). He explained that empathy should be understood as an advanced cognitive process that is both emotional and intellectual. From an emotional standpoint, "empathy is widely referred to as empathic concern." According to Warren, "empathic concern represents the feelings of sympathy, personal closeness, grief, and/or the emotional human connection of the observer to the target" (p. 398). In other words, a teacher who possesses empathic concern has an internal alarm clock that will alert her to respond to the needs of students. For example, a teacher might overhear a student telling one of his close friends that his parents are going through a divorce. In response to hearing the news, the teacher may conference privately with the student at the end of class to intentionally offer encouragement and emotional support. This response is fueled by the teacher's empathic concern. The teacher might explicitly say, "I just want you to know that I am here for you if you need someone to talk to. I will also set up a meeting with the school counselor if you do not feel comfortable talking to me about the situation. I just want to make sure you get the support you need." Warren (2013) explains that "empathic concern includes feelings of sorrow and personal distress based on the perception of one's suffering or unfortunate circumstances" (p. 398).

Empathy is displayed not only by an emotional response but also by an intellectual response. From an intellectual standpoint, "empathy is termed perspective taking" (Warren, 2013, p. 398). According to Warren, perspective-taking has two modalities:

1. "Imagine Other" – the ability to imagine how another person is experiencing his or her condition.
2. "Imagine Self" – the ability to imagine how one's own self would personally experience another person's condition.

These concepts are best summarized by the proverb, "Walk a mile in someone else's shoes." To strategically employ empathic concern or perspective-taking, educators might ask themselves the following questions: How are my students feeling at this present moment? Do they feel confident and capable? What can I do to motivate my students? Do my students feel anxious, joyful, angry, or inspired? If I were in my students' position, how would I feel? If I were a student enrolled in a Title 1 school, how difficult would it be for me to prioritize academic success while my family struggles with food or housing insecurity?

Genuine attempts by educators to understand the students they intend to serve require empathy. We can cultivate empathic concern and perspective-taking to develop a more empathic teaching disposition. These concepts can help educators demonstrate the level of empathy needed to employ culturally responsive practices effectively.

Strategy #2 – Culturally Responsive Teaching Self-Efficacy (CRTSE)

Despite mounting empirical evidence compiled over decades highlighting the positive impact culturally responsive teaching has on student achievement and engagement (Abacioglu et al., 2020; Aronson and Laughter, 2016; Byrd, 2016; Gay, 2018; Hammond, 2015; J. Irvine, 1990; Ladson-Billings, 1994), many educators in today's classrooms lack the confidence and efficacy required to effectively employ a culturally responsive approach to teaching and learning.

One researcher, Dr. Kamou Siwatu, explored factors that contribute to low levels of culturally responsive teaching self-efficacy (CRTSE). Siwatu et al. (2016) "examined preservice teachers' culturally responsive teaching self-efficacy doubts and how they explained the sources of these doubts" (p. 290). By interviewing eight preservice teachers enrolled in an undergraduate teacher preparation program, Siwatu et al. (2016) found that preservice educators were least efficacious in their ability to perform the following culturally responsive teaching tasks:

1. Design a lesson that shows how other cultural groups have made use of mathematics.
2. Identify ways that standardized tests may be biased toward linguistically diverse students.
3. Identify ways that standardized tests may be biased toward culturally diverse students.
4. Communicate with the parents of English Language Learners regarding their child's achievement.
5. Teach students about their cultures' contributions to science.

(p. 284)

While Siwatu et al.'s work focused on preservice educators who lacked classroom experience, I conducted a similar study in 2022 to explore the relationship between in-service educators' multicultural consciousness and CRTSE. The findings from my quantitative study confirmed Siwatu and colleagues' findings, as 112 in-service educators also indicated that they were least efficacious to: 1) design a lesson that shows how other cultural groups have made use of mathematics, 2) communicate with the parents of English Language Learners regarding their child's achievement, and 3) teach students about their culture's contribution to science (Taylor, 2022). The implications of these two studies indicate a need to build educator confidence and efficacy to employ a culturally responsive approach in the learning environment.

In Siwatu et al.'s (2016) study, the authors explained that educators believed the culturally responsive teaching strategy would work, yet they did not believe they could execute the strategy successfully. When interviewed about the sources of their doubts, the educators acknowledged that their self-efficacy doubts stemmed from "a general lack of knowledge regarding student diversity and culturally responsive pedagogy" (Siwatu et al., 2016, p. 286). Educators also acknowledged that they lacked exposure to diverse cultures and, therefore, did not possess "any knowledge about different cultures' contributions to science or mathematics" (p. 286). It is clear that educators need assistance developing their understanding of diverse contributions across the curriculum. In addition, educators would benefit from support that would specifically increase their confidence to work with culturally diverse students and families.

Siwatu et al. (2016) recommended two intervention strategies to help educators gain confidence in their ability to apply culturally responsive teaching strategies. The first recommendation involves helping educators develop the "declarative, procedural, and conditional knowledge related to culturally responsive pedagogy" (p. 292). This intervention aims to build educators' capacity to perform culturally responsive tasks. The second recommendation is to provide educators with opportunities to nurture self-efficacy beliefs.

Strategy #3 – Collective Culturally Responsive Teacher Efficacy (CCRTE)

Collective culturally responsive teacher efficacy (CCRTE) is a new concept that I am introducing to educational literature. I define it as "the collective belief that educators in a given school can improve the academic and behavioral outcomes of culturally diverse students." Like CRTSE, CCRTE emerges from Albert Bandura's (1993) self-efficacy theory. Additionally, it is heavily influenced by the work of Megan Tschannen-Moran and Marilyn Barr (2004), John Hattie (2016), and Jennifer Donohoo (2017). Tschannen-Moran and Barr (2004) explained that collective teacher efficacy "refers to the collective perception that teachers in a given school make an educational difference to their students over and above the educational impact of their homes and communities" (p. 190). It is not an isolated view of each teacher's efficacy but rather a collective view of the combined efficacy of teachers in a school as a single unit.

Tschannen-Moran and Barr's work highlighted the benefits of collective teacher efficacy. The school staff with a high level of collective teacher efficacy believe that students are teachable and can be motivated to achieve high levels across subject areas. This is because collective teacher efficacy impacts how teachers deliver instruction and respond to behavioral concerns within the school setting. According to Tschannen-Moran and Barr (2004), "Collective teacher efficacy influences student achievement because greater efficacy leads to greater effort and persistence, which results in better performance" (p. 191).

It is important to underscore that this concept of collective teacher efficacy is based on teachers' beliefs in their own abilities. Donohoo asserts, "When teachers believe that together they and their colleagues can impact student achievement, they share a sense of collective teacher efficacy" (p. 3). In essence, educators in schools who demonstrate collective teacher efficacy believe that they cause academic success. Hence, CCRTE takes this exact concept and applies it directly to the education of culturally diverse students. Therefore, the most important question to ask when inquiring about CCRTE in a given school is this: Can we increase the academic performance of culturally diverse students in our school? Does my school have the CCRTE required to improve outcomes for Black students, Hispanic students, Asian students, and other minority populations?

CCRTE not only challenges the efficacy beliefs of individual teachers, but it also challenges the culturally responsive efficacy beliefs of every adult working in a particular school context. I believe culturally diverse students must be centered when discussing teacher efficacy because many teachers are more efficacious in meeting the needs of mainstream students (i.e., white, middle-class students) when compared to culturally diverse students (Siwatu et al., 2016; Taylor, 2022). I argue that any school committed to fostering the efficacy beliefs of educators teaching culturally diverse students will increase the likelihood of closing academic achievement gaps, which has been a focus of educational researchers for decades (Williams, 2011).

According to Donohoo (2017), "Efficacy beliefs are very powerful because they guide educators' actions and behavior. Efficacy beliefs help determine what educators focus on, how they respond to challenges, and how they expend their efforts" (p. xv). Furthermore, Donohoo (2017) asserts that educators with high efficacy demonstrate the following traits:

1. Show greater effort and persistence
2. Are more willing to try new teaching approaches
3. Pay more attention to students who are falling behind
4. Convey high expectations for students
5. Foster learner autonomy
6. Welcome increased parental involvement (p. xv)

Additionally, if we desire to increase the academic performance of diverse students and close achievement gaps, we must commit to cultivating CCRTE. Culturally diverse students deserve efficacious educators.

Fostering Efficacy Beliefs

In 2009, John Hattie published *Visible Learning: A Synthesis of Over 800 Meta-Analyses Related to Achievement*. He sought to determine which factors, out of hundreds, had the greatest impact on student achievement. Hattie then ranked those factors based on their effect size (i.e., the strength of the relationship between two variables). Hattie concluded that collective teacher efficacy is at the top of the ranking. This means that it is one of the most significant predictors of student achievement (Hattie, 2009). (For more information about Hattie's work, please visit https://visible-learning.org/2018/03/collective-teacher-efficacy-hattie/.)

Mastery Experiences

In her work around fostering efficacy beliefs, Donohoo (2017) explains that "Four sources shaping collective efficacy beliefs include mastery experiences, vicarious experiences, social persuasion, and affective states" (p. 8). Due to the limitations of this book, I will only focus on the top two most powerful sources of collective efficacy: Mastery experiences and vicarious experiences. According to Donohoo, the most powerful source of collective teacher efficacy is mastery experiences, which can be fostered when a team or group of teachers experience success (mastery) and attribute that success to their own actions.

Example A: Fostering Mastery Experiences

Sarah, a ninth-grade English teacher, and three colleagues from her department have constantly struggled to maintain student engagement during English class. Yet, after attending a workshop about creating culturally responsive writing lessons, they collaborated to design a lesson based on their students' lived experiences, interests, and preferences. The teachers were determined to incorporate knowledge about their students' identities and cultures into the lesson plan. Additionally, they all agreed to utilize a poem as an anticipatory set to introduce the concept of creative writing because their students are self-proclaimed "hip-hop heads" (i.e., individuals enamored with hip-hop music). After planning together, each teacher went to their individual classrooms to administer the lesson. Sarah gave her students the journal prompt that required them to describe popular metaphors they identified in their favorite songs. Once instructions were given, Sarah immediately noticed that 100% of her students were engaged and working diligently on the assignment.

When Sarah returned to her department meeting to explain the success of her lesson, she found out that each of the teachers who administered the culturally responsive writing assignment experienced success as well. This example illustrates a mastery experience. Together, they have increased their collective culturally responsive teaching efficacy because they know it was their willingness to employ culturally responsive practices that led to increased student engagement.

Vicarious Experiences

Donohoo (2017) explains that "The second most powerful source of collective efficacy is vicarious experiences" (p. 8). Unlike mastery experiences, vicarious experiences do not require educators to experience personal success. However, teachers can experience vicarious experiences when they witness or learn about the success of other educators. For example, while not every English teacher in Sarah's school engaged their students in a culturally responsive writing assignment, hearing about Sarah's success might increase their confidence and efficacy in employing culturally responsive practices in the English classroom. Their efficacy may increase due to the vicarious experience shared with them about Sarah and her colleagues. Donohoo (2017) believes vicarious experiences "can occur through site visits, watching videos, networking, or reading about it" (p. 8).

Summary

In summary, teachers must center students' cultural backgrounds in the academic space. Culture permeates every aspect of students' lives and strongly influences how students view academic content. It is only prudent for educators to leverage students' cultural backgrounds to maximize learning.

Reflective Questions for Chapter 2

Do you think it is important for educators to develop an understanding of culture as it relates to students' identities? What could happen to a student's self-esteem if an educator created an atmosphere in the classroom that devalued or neglected students' cultures? What could happen to a student's self-esteem if an educator made them feel as if their culture were valued and accepted in the classroom? Are you willing to increase your multicultural awareness by exploring resources that highlight the significant contributions of diverse scientists, inventors, mathematicians, writers, entrepreneurs, etc.? What professional learning opportunities do you believe could possibly help you foster culturally responsive teaching self-efficacy through vicarious experiences? Are you committed to the process of becoming a culturally responsive educator? (For a more in-depth understanding of this process, I recommend my book, titled *Becoming Culturally Responsive Educators: 5 Necessary Action Steps*).

As we strive to become culturally responsive educators, our aim must be to ensure that every child feels seen, heard, valued, and empowered. The goal isn't just to nurture academic growth; the goal must also include fostering social and emotional development. It is the responsibility of educators to establish an environment that celebrates diversity, promotes equity, and prepares our students to navigate and thrive in a multicultural world.

Review of Summarized Findings from This Chapter:

1. It is important for educators to understand how to remove the barriers of deficit thinking and cultural mismatch as they may hinder the academic achievement of culturally diverse students.
2. Effective culturally responsive practitioners are committed to developing an appreciation for cultural diversity by reading materials that highlight the contributions of diverse peoples in mathematics, science, and other academic disciplines.
3. Teachers must embrace empathy as a teaching disposition.
4. Practicing empathic concern and perspective-taking can help cultivate empathy within the context of school.
5. Research has proven that employing culturally responsive teaching practices can meet the diverse needs of all learners.
6. Intentionally seeking to build self-efficacy and the collective efficacy of every adult within a school setting can increase student achievement.
   a. According to Donohoo et al. (2018), "School leaders must work to build a culture designed to increase collective teacher efficacy, which will affect teachers' behavior and student beliefs" (p. 44).
   b. Tschannen-Moran and Barr (2004) state, "Teachers in schools with high collective efficacy do not accept low student achievement as an inevitable byproduct of low socioeconomic status, lack of ability, or family background. They roll up their sleeves and get the job done" (p. 192).
7. Do not be afraid to try a new teaching strategy. Fear can become a barrier to your mastery experience.

References

Aaronson, D., Barrow, L., & Sander, W. (2007). Teachers and student achievement in the Chicago public high schools. *Journal of Labor Economics, 25*(1), 95–135.

Abacioglu, C. S., Volman, M., & Fischer, A. H. (2020). Teachers' multicultural attitudes and perspective-taking abilities as factors in culturally responsive teaching. *British Journal of Educational Psychology, 90*, 736–752. https://doi.org/10.1111/bjep.12328

Aronson, B. & Laughter, J. (2016). The theory and practice of culturally relevant education: A synthesis of research across content areas. *Review of Educational Research, 86*(1), 163–206. https://doi.org/10.3102%2F0034654315582066

Bandura, A. (1993). Perceived self-efficacy in cognitive development and functioning. *Educational Psychologist, 28*(2), 117–148.

Byrd, C. M. (2016). Does culturally relevant teaching work? An examination from student perspectives. *SAGE Open, 6*(3). https://doi.org/10.1177/2158244016660744

Causadias, J. (2020). What is culture? Systems of people, places, and practices. *Applied Developmental Science, 24*, 310–322.

Chu, S. (2016). Developing a scale to investigate in-service special education teacher efficacy for serving students from culturally and linguistically diverse backgrounds. *Journal of Curriculum and Teaching, 5*(1), 39–51. http://dx.doi.org/10.5430/jct.v5n1p39

Coritz, A., Pena, J., Jacobs, P., Rico, B., Hahn, J., & Lowe, H. J. (2023, September 21). Census Bureau releases 2020 census population for more than 200 new detailed race and ethnicity groups. The United States Census. https://www.census.gov/library/stories/2023/09/2020-census-dhc-a-race-overview.html

Donohoo, J. (2017). *Collective efficacy: How educators' beliefs impact student learning*. Corwin.

Donohoo, J., Hattie, J., & Eells, R. (2018). The power of collective efficacy. *Educational Leadership, 75*, 40–44.

Dudley-Marling, C. (2015). The resilience of deficit thinking. *Journal of Teaching and Learning, 10*(1), 1–12. https://doi.org/10.22329/jtl.v10i1.4171

Fuller, A. (2021). *Overcoming cultural mismatch: Reaching and teaching diverse children*. Rowman & Littlefield.

Gay, G. (2018). *Culturally responsive teaching: Theory, research, and practice* (3rd ed.). Teachers College Press.

Hammond, Z. L. (2015). *Culturally responsive teaching and the brain: Promoting authentic engagement and rigor among culturally and linguistically diverse students*. Corwin.

Hattie, J. (2009). *Visible learning: A synthesis of 800+ meta-analyses on achievement*. Routledge.

Hattie, J. (2016). Third Visible Learning Annual Conference: Mindframes and Maximizers, Washington, DC, July 11.

Irvine, J. (1990). *Black students and school failure*. Greenwood.

Irvine, J. J. (2009). Relevant beyond the basics. *Teaching Tolerance, 36*, 41–44. https://www.learningforjustice.org/magazine/fall-2009/relevant-beyond-the-basics

Irvine, J. J. (2012). Complex relationships between multicultural education and special education: An African American perspective. *Journal of Teacher Education, 63*(4), 268–274.

Jandt, F. E. (2004). *Intercultural communication: A global reader*. Sage Publications.

Keefer, N. (2017). The presence of deficit thinking among social studies educators. *Journal of Social Studies Education Research, 8*(3), 50–75.

Kozlowski, K. P. (2015). Culture or teacher bias? Racial and ethnic variation in student-teacher effort assessment match/mismatch. *Race and Social Problems, 7*(1), 43–59. https://doi.org/10.1007/s12552-014-9138-x

Ladson-Billings, G. (1994). *The dreamkeepers: Successful teachers of African American children*. Jossey-Bass.

McGrady, P. B. & Reynolds, J. R. (2013). Racial mismatch in the classroom: Beyond black-white differences: A magazine of theory and practice. *Sociology of Education, 86*(1), 3–17. http://dx.doi.org/10.1177/0038040712444857

Patton Davis, L. & Museus, S. (2019). What is deficit thinking? An analysis of conceptualizations of deficit thinking and implications for scholarly research. *Currents, 1*(1), 117–130. http://dx.doi.org/10.3998/currents.17387731.0001.110

Pollack, T. M. (2012). The miseducation of a beginning teacher: One educator's critical reflections on the functions and power of deficit narratives. *Multicultural Perspectives, 14*(2), 93–98. https://doi.org/10.1080/15210960.2012.673318

Recknagel, C., Hong, J., Francis, D. C., Wang, Q., Parsons, A., & Lewis, L. (2022). The wrong tools for the job: Teachers' voices on cultural capital mismatch. *International Journal of Multicultural Education*, *24*(2), 57–79. https://doi.org/10.18251/ijme.v24i2.2533

Samovar, L. A., Porter, R. E., and McDaniel, E. R. (2012). *Intercultural communication: A reader* (13th ed.). Wadsworth Cengage Learning.

Siwatu, K. O., Chesnut, S. R., Alejandro, A. Y., & Young, H. A. (2016). Examining preservice teachers' culturally responsive teaching self-efficacy doubts. *The Teacher Educator*, *51*(4), 277–296. https://doi.org/10.1080/08878730.2016.1192709

Taylor, J. H. (2022). Relationship between multicultural consciousness and culturally responsive teaching self-efficacy (Order No. 30241427). Available from *ProQuest Dissertations & Theses Global*. (2753378936). https://go.openathens.net/redirector/liberty.edu?url=https://www.proquest.com/dissertations-theses/relationship-between-multicultural-consciousness/docview/2753378936/se-2

Tschannen-Moran, M. & Barr, M. (2004). Fostering student learning: The relationship of collective teacher efficacy and student achievement. *Leadership and Policy in Schools*, *3*, 189–209. 10.1080/15700760490503706.

U.S. Department of Education. (2016). The state of racial diversity in the educator workforce. https://www.2.ed.gov/rschstat/eval/highered/racial-diversity/state-racial-diversity-workforce.pdf

Valenzuela, A. (1999). *Subtractive schooling: U.S.-Mexican youth and the politics of caring*. State University of New York Press.

Warren, C. (2013). Towards a pedagogy for the application of empathy in culturally diverse classrooms. *The Urban Review*, *46*, 395–419.

What is cultural mismatch in Education? (2019, February 27). Cultural mismatch in education. https://www.culturalmismatch.org/about/

White, L. A. (2022, August 5). Culture. Encyclopedia Britannica. https://www.britannica.com/topic/culture

Williams, A. (2011). A call for change: Narrowing the achievement gap between white and minority students. *The Clearing House*, *84*(2), 65–71. https://doi.org/10.1080/00098655.2010.511308

3

The "E" in I.C.E.D. T.E.A.

Empowerment

"Some Students Need an Empowering Teacher"

I was 13 years old when I entered high school as a ninth-grade student. By this time in my life, I was disinterested in academic achievement and ultimately disengaged from school. I had severe attendance issues, and my grade point average (GPA) was abysmal. To be exact, I had a 0.75 GPA, I had been marked absent from school 16 days, and I had been marked tardy to class nine times. I simply did not like school. I did not see school as a place where I could thrive. Therefore, when I showed up, I was more focused on socializing and showing off my outfits than demonstrating my academic potential. My outfit usually included a pair of dark blue jeans, a white tee shirt, a gold chain, a gray beanie hat, and some pristine, white Nike Air Force 1's. I was fresh! I was prepared for whatever the day required, except demonstrating my ability to master academic concepts.

As I stated earlier, I did not like school. It was not something I felt empowered to engage in. Although I had some good teachers throughout my life, I needed teachers who were ready and willing to empower me to learn. My unique background, upbringing, and lived experiences molded me into a student requiring teachers who commanded the classroom with a compassionate presence. I needed teachers who spoke with conviction as they challenged my expectations for myself. I did not necessarily need "tough love"; I needed someone genuine and authentic in their belief in my potential. I needed someone who could see my academic capabilities and explicitly communicate those capabilities to me to inspire me to reach my potential. I needed an empowering teacher.

As an educator, I have learned that many students need an empowering teacher. An empowering teacher is a teacher who uses communication techniques to persuade students to believe in their intellectual power. These are the educators who know how to get the most effort out of seemingly the most challenging students. As a former teacher of students with emotional and behavioral challenges, an empowering pedagogical disposition was required to help my students achieve academic success. As a former Title 1 Instructional Coach, I have helped countless teachers understand that some students require a pedagogy that is inclusive of empowerment. The reality is that some students will never demonstrate the inherent brilliance they possess without educators who are committed to empowering them to succeed at a high level.

Empowering Students

In this chapter, I argue that teachers need to know to what extent their students need to be empowered. The language of *empowering* students is not new to educational literature. Thirty years ago, an academic researcher and author named Dr. Gloria Ladson-Billings (1994) explained that teachers could increase the performance of Black students by employing a pedagogy that "empowers students intellectually, socially, emotionally, and politically using cultural referents to impart knowledge, skills, and attitudes" (pp. 16–17). She called this approach culturally relevant pedagogy. Dr. Ladson-Billings found that effective teachers of Black students demonstrated an ability to empower students.

> To empower students, educators must be willing to intentionally help students feel more powerful in the academic setting.

To empower students, educators must be willing to intentionally help students feel more powerful in the academic setting. This might look like authorizing students to use their voices in the learning environment to express their perspectives and opinions without fear of failure or rejection. It might look like explicitly giving students permission to show up to school as their authentic, brilliant selves. Additionally, empowering students might look like building students' confidence and agency to complete complex and rigorous academic tasks. The goal of empowering students is to help them become as independent as possible.

When students are empowered, they increase their belief in their own intellectual power and ability. An empowered student also develops the mental strength and fortitude to develop the persistence needed to

> When students are empowered, they increase their belief in their own intellectual power and ability.

succeed in and out of school. Although all students can benefit from having access to an empowering educator, most will not be empowered as long as educators adopt a pedagogy that is absent of empowerment. For this reason, this chapter elevates the role of empowerment as a practical pedagogical disposition and instructional tool in the K–12 setting.

Empowerment and Self-Efficacy

I argue that there is a relationship between empowerment and self-efficacy. I believe strongly in the notion that an empowered learner is an efficacious learner, and an efficacious learner is an empowered learner. Thus, educators must see empowerment as a tool to increase student efficacy. Albert Bandura's (1977) germinal work around self-efficacy theory defined self-efficacy as "beliefs in one's capabilities to organize and execute the courses of action required to produce given attainments" (p. 3). In other words, self-efficacy is a person's belief in their own ability to get something done. When we apply this concept to students, we understand that students who do not believe in their abilities to solve complex mathematical equations lack self-efficacy in math. When a student internalizes the idea that he or she is not a strong reader, we must interpret this through the lens of reading efficacy. Students who lack confidence in their reading ability are likely to avoid the task of reading. This means they are unlikely to commit to the process of becoming a better reader. This is why helping students develop self-efficacy is important. It is necessary for improvement. Once we see student academic performance through the lens of efficacy, we will realize that empowerment is a strategy to improve students' efficacy, which ultimately will improve students' overall performance.

As mentioned in the previous chapter, "efficacy beliefs impact how people feel, think, act, and motivate themselves" (Tschannen-Moran & Barr, 2004, p. 190). Therefore, whenever a teacher comes across an uninspired, unmotivated, or disengaged student, that educator has just encountered someone who would benefit from an empowering educator. The question is, how many teachers possess a pedagogy of empowerment? How many teachers have the capacity to empower students in such a way that students become more efficacious to perform rigorous academic tasks? How many teachers are willing to employ a pedagogy of empowerment to help students develop academic confidence?

According to Donohoo (2017), "students' estimates of their own performance (also known as students' expectations), prior achievement, and motivation" influence their achievement (p. 4). In other words, how students see themselves impacts their performance. This is why the I.C.E.D. T.E.A. Framework is critical. It begins the process of centering students' identities first. Then, we move toward understanding students' cultural backgrounds. Once we have a foundational understanding of students' identities and cultures, we progress toward a pedagogy that includes empowerment. Educators must be willing and able to help students believe in their own potential. Then, educators must be committed to helping students demonstrate behavior that aligns with their newly elevated expectations for themselves.

To bolster students' belief in themselves, teachers must intentionally seek to empower students. While we can assume that some students will enter the school feeling empowered and confident, we can also assume that many others will not. Some students will refuse to read aloud, ask questions, or complete rigorous tasks without the support of an adult. These students have not developed the confidence required to independently complete rigorous assignments at a high level. Therefore, these are the students who are most in need of empowerment. Unmotivated students need to develop the confidence and efficacy needed to thrive independently in and out of school. Now, let's talk about three strategies that can be employed to empower students.

Three Strategies for Empowering Students
Strategy #1 – Speaking Life
"Speaking Life" refers to the intentional act of communicating words that uplift, motivate, and inspire hope. While this strategy may not be ubiquitous in educational literature, it is steeped in the traditions of the historical Black church in America. As a young man attending church, I frequently heard adults "speaking life" to children. I remember being present during a Sunday school lesson where a young child expressed doubt in his ability to recite a Bible passage. With a dejected facial expression, he simply stated, "I can't do it." Yet, before he could finish lamenting and expressing doubt, the Sunday school teacher looked him directly in the face and encouraged him by saying, "You can do it. You have what it takes. You are smart. So, let's try this again." Then, the young child was prompted again to recite the passage, which he did successfully.

The Sunday School teacher's intentional use of words to inspire effort is known as speaking life. Although speaking life may seem like an easy strategy to employ, the educator who desires to speak life to students must possess enough empathy and charisma to be persuasive. As a student, I had several educators who spoke life into me on a personal level. One teacher who comes to mind is Mr. Jobie Boone. Mr. Boone was my fourth-grade teacher at G. W. Carver Intermediate. He was the only African American male teacher I had ever had during my K–12 experience. He was firm, fair, and empowering. On several occasions, Mr. Boone would ask me to step out of the classroom so he could have a few words with me. He would say, "Jahkari, you are an intelligent young man. You have what it takes to be successful, but you have to work harder in my class. I believe in you. Now, let's go. It's time to get it together."

At that stage of my life, I was more committed to being the class clown than an honor roll student. Yet, Mr. Boone saw something in me that I struggled to see within myself. He saw potential. Not only did he see my potential, but he also explicitly told me about it. He used his words to encourage and challenge me to become a better student every day. He epitomized the concept of speaking life. Mr. Boone explicitly used his words to encourage me to put more effort into my classes. He communicated a vision of academic success for me that I struggled to see. Nevertheless, by consistently taking the time to speak life to me, Mr. Boone inspired me to take my academics seriously.

Consider struggling learners. Consider the student who has been identified as having a specific learning disability. Consider how many times they have been explicitly reminded of their impairments. Opposed to being a recipient of words intentionally designed to uplift, motivate, and inspire hope, that student has been constantly informed about what they cannot do. This is the type of child who will need to be empowered by an educator who can speak life into them.

Also, consider the student who has experienced the emotional toll of childhood trauma. Maybe that child has been neglected. Maybe that child has witnessed a tragic event that has left him grappling with high levels of anxiety. That same child is expected to enter the school, carrying the invisible baggage of emotional scars and still perform at a high academic level. This will be difficult, especially if that child is never engaged by an educator who is willing to intentionally communicate words that empower and heal. Speaking life is a strategy for uplifting children emotionally, mentally, and psychologically, not just academically. Some students will require this empowering and holistic pedagogical approach in order to make academic progress.

Strategy #2 – Family Engagement

The second strategy for empowering students is to commit to family engagement. Mapp et al. (2022) define family engagement as "A full, equal, and equitable partnership among families, educators, and community partners to promote children's learning and development from birth through college and career" (p. 16). According to Mapp et al. (2022), family engagement improves student achievement, mental health, and graduation rates. It is also linked to significant gains in reading and math. Therefore, family engagement must be considered an effective strategy for empowering students.

Educators looking to engage families can start by establishing strong, trusting relationships with students' families. In a study on the impact of "Structured Conversations about Learning" between teachers and parents, Humphrey and Squires (2011) found that students' self-confidence, motivation, and academic achievement increased as teachers fostered deeper relationships with families. By engaging families, educators can provide parents and guardians with new insight and information that allows them to encourage their children's learning and development at home in a way that is aligned with how learning and development are enriched at school. Humphrey and Squires (2011) describe a teacher reporting that one of the students started believing in his capabilities as an achiever as a result of coordinated family engagement. Ultimately, engaging the student's family improved literacy performance, as evidenced by writing scores. Humphrey and Squires's work provides one example of how engaging families can effectively empower students academically.

Strategy #3 – Academic Feedback

The third strategy for empowering students is to offer quality feedback that helps them understand what they need to do to make academic gains. According to Hattie and Timperley (2007), "feedback is one of the most powerful influences on learning and achievement, but this impact can be either positive or negative" (p. 81). In other words, feedback is most certainly powerful enough to move the academic needle. However, we must ask ourselves if the feedback we provide is moving the academic needle toward progression, or, in reverse, toward regression. Educators must understand that feedback can be constructive or destructive. It can empower students to put forth their best effort or discourage them from achieving their potential. Therefore, educators must strive to embrace feedback as a strategy designed to encourage learning and achievement. While teachers can provide students with numerous types of feedback for brevity's sake, I am speaking solely of academic feedback.

Academic feedback refers to providing students with information in response to their performance on an academic task or assignment. Teachers can give students a grade or score on an assignment as a means of feedback. Teachers can also provide students with academic feedback via written comments, stickers, facial expressions, etc. Yet, we want to make sure that the feedback that is provided can move the academic needle in a positive direction. According to the University of South Carolina's Center for Teaching Excellence (2024), "The purpose of feedback in the assessment and learning process is to improve a student's performance – not put a damper on it. It is essential that the process of providing feedback is a positive, or at least a neutral, learning experience for the student." By answering the following three questions from a posture of empowering students, teachers can provide students with meaningful academic feedback:

1. What can the student do?
2. In what academic area does the student need to make improvements?
3. What does the student need to do to make progress or demonstrate growth in that area?

By providing students with feedback that answers the three aforementioned questions, educators increase the likelihood of students making academic progress.

Reflective Questions for Chapter 3

What if all students had access to educators who employed a pedagogy of empowerment? Consider students with disabilities and others who are often marginalized in the academic setting. Would students be more or less likely to demonstrate engagement if they had access to adults who empowered them? Would students be more or less likely to increase their personal confidence and self-determination skills if they had access to empowering educators? How might achievement gaps be influenced by a collective group of educators who demonstrated a pedagogy of empowerment? How might culturally diverse students be influenced by educators on a mission to intentionally empower them? Considering Dr. Gloria Ladson-Billings's work on culturally relevant pedagogy, is it possible to be culturally responsive without a pedagogy of empowerment? Ladson-Billings defined culturally relevant pedagogy as one that "*empowers* students intellectually, socially, emotionally, and politically using cultural referents to impart knowledge, skills, and attitudes" (emphasis added, pp. 16–17).

In today's schools, educators are likely to encounter students who appear disengaged, deflated, or unmotivated in the academic setting. The question we must ask is, when this occurs, how will we respond? Will we send the student to an administrator with a referral that details non-compliant behaviors, or will we employ a pedagogy of empowerment to help the student develop self-confidence and agency? I argue that educators must respond with a pedagogy of empowerment. Any educator capable of empowering students will ultimately place students in the best position to be successful in and out of school.

Review of Summarized Findings from This Chapter:

1. Culturally relevant pedagogy refers to a pedagogy that "empowers students intellectually, socially, emotionally, and politically using cultural referents to impart knowledge, skills, and attitudes" (Ladson-Billings, 1994, pp. 16–17).
2. Empowering students can look like building students' confidence and agency to complete complex and rigorous academic tasks.
3. Educators must see empowerment as a tool to increase student efficacy.
4. Strategies for empowering students include:
    a. *Speaking Life* – "Speaking Life" refers to the intentional act of communicating words that uplift, motivate, and inspire hope. Some students need educators who will speak life and encourage them to see their potential.
    b. *Family Engagement* – One of the most effective ways to empower students is to commit to family engagement. Prioritizing students' families and communities and seeking their input and perspective can be empowering for students.
    c. *Academic Feedback* – This refers to providing students with information in response to their performance on an academic task or assignment. Provide students with meaningful feedback that will empower them to persist on their academic journey and continually make improvements.

References

Bandura, A. (1977). Self-efficacy: Toward a unifying theory of behavioral change. *Psychological Review, 84*(2), 191–215.

Bandura, A. (1993). Perceived self-efficacy in cognitive development and functioning. *Educational Psychologist, 28*(2), 117–148.

Donohoo, J. (2017). *Collective efficacy: How educators' beliefs impact student learning.* Corwin.

Hattie, J. (1999, August). Influences on student learning (Inaugural professorial address, University of Auckland, New Zealand). https://geoffpetty.com/wp-content/uploads/2012/12/Influencesonstudent2C683.pdf

Hattie, J. (2009). *Visible learning: A synthesis of 800+ meta-analyses on achievement.* Routledge.

Hattie, J. (2016). Third Visible Learning Annual Conference: Mindframes and Maximizers, Washington, DC, July 11.

Hattie, J. & Timperley, H. (2007). The power of feedback. *Review of Educational Research, 77*(1), 81–112.

Humphrey, N. & Squires, G. (2011). Achievement for all national evaluation: Final report. https://api.core.ac.uk/oai/oai:pure.atira.dk:publications/83cbeae4-4c5a-4ad6-ac02-0ea3eed6aea4

Ladson-Billings, G. (1994). *The dreamkeepers: Successful teachers of African American children.* Jossey-Bass.

Mapp, K., Henderson, A., Cuevas, S., Franco, M., & Ewert, S. (2022). *Everyone wins! The evidence for family-school partnerships & implications for practice.* Scholastic.

Tschannen-Moran, M. & Barr, M. (2004). Fostering student learning: The relationship of collective teacher efficacy and student achievement. *Leadership and Policy in Schools, 3*, 189–209.

University of South Carolina. (2024). Importance of providing meaningful student feedback. University of South Carolina Center for Teaching Excellence. https://sc.edu/about/offices_and_divisions/cte/teaching_resources/grading_assessment_toolbox/providing_meaningful_student_feedback/index.php

4

The "D" in I.C.E.D. T.E.A.

Dreams

While "dreams" are often associated with thoughts, images, or unconscious experiences that occur while a person is asleep, in this chapter, I define dreams as *strong desires, goals, or future aspirations that a person wishes to accomplish*. In other words, dreams are personal ambitions. They represent what a person intends to achieve or become in life. From that perspective, we must understand that a person's dreams carry significant details about their identity. I believe every person has dreams that spring forth from the depths of their core, especially children. In fact, some dreams originate during childhood when a child's imagination is hyperactive. These dreams are deeply rooted, personal, and precious to the dreamer. When a teacher makes an attempt to understand the dreams of a student, that teacher is making an attempt to build deep rapport with a student and learn about the students' future aspirations. Since dreams reveal what a person values and holds dear to their heart, encouraging children to dream and express their dreams should be promoted in school.

> I define dreams as *strong desires, goals, or future aspirations that a person wishes to accomplish*. In other words, dreams are personal ambitions. They represent what a person intends to achieve or become in life.

DOI: 10.4324/9781003613626-5

Dr. Christopher Emdin, the Maxine Greene Chair for Distinguished Contributions to Education and Professor of Science Education at Teachers College, Columbia University, is a champion for encouraging students to dream. In his recent book titled *Stem, Steam, Make, Dream* (2022), Dr. Emdin encourages school leaders to engage in the work of creating a "Dream Culture" (p. 102). Emdin states, "Dream Culture is about recommitting to the dream of thriving schools for the sake of our children's futures (p. 103). He further explains that "A Dream Culture is a lived reality that privileges a way of thinking and doing that pushes the boundaries of normality by encouraging the imagination and manifesting what it produces" (p. 103). Can you imagine a powerful literacy lesson that encourages students to write an essay rooted in dreams that push the boundaries of what is considered normal? Can you imagine empowering students to dream of new ways to strengthen and ultimately transform their communities? Dreams can be transformative tools to engage and motivate students.

Leveraging Dreams to Strengthen Relationships

Dreams, as aspirations, help to reveal what a person values and deems meaningful and worthy of pursuit. Caroline Hart, Professor and Lecturer in Education Studies at the University of Sheffield in the United Kingdom, states, "Aspirations matter as signifiers of what has come to have meaning and value for us, as individuals, or as social groups" (2016, p. 336). In other words, dreams are not just important to individuals, but they are also important to the social groups in which individuals belong. This can be insightful for understanding students, their peer groups, their families, and the communities they belong to.

For example, consider the student who plans to enroll in a high school Reserve Officers' Training Corp (ROTC) because of a dream to enter the military. The dream could be inspired by a desire to follow in the footsteps of family members who have demonstrated generations of service history. This means that the student's dream is connected to the identity of the social group in which she belongs. Knowing students' dreams can provide us with knowledge of what the student values and it may also help educators develop an understanding of the student's family values. This insight can help educators spark a conversation that begins the relationship and rapport-building process.

Educators can leverage knowledge of students' dreams to establish a personal connection with students and their families. For example, as a student growing up in an impoverished neighborhood, I dreamed of purchasing a house for my mother and moving her to a safer neighborhood. By offering me an opportunity to share my dreams and aspirations, the educator would learn a great deal about my love and affinity for my mother and my desire to ensure her safety. Once the educator possesses that knowledge, they can leverage that insight to connect with me on a deeper level through brief conversations centered around my dream of providing a better life for myself and my family.

The educator could speak with me about strategies for bringing my dream to fruition (staying in school, learning about real estate, etc.). In addition, the educator could use that knowledge to facilitate the family engagement process. Strategically and intentionally, the educator could call my mother to express how I shared my dream of relocating her to a safer community. From that conversation, the educator can develop a partnership with my mother to maximize my performance in school in an attempt to help me get closer to my dreams and aspirations. How do you think that conversation would make my mother feel? Her heart would be warmed to hear how her child desires to take care of her. These conversations, centered around a student's dreams, can build positive rapport between educators, students, and families.

Leveraging Dreams for Academic Connections

In addition to leveraging students' dreams to establish and enhance positive rapport, educators can use knowledge of students' dreams to connect what students value to academic content. For example, if a middle school student shares her dream of attending an Ivy League university, her teacher could use that insight to further the student's knowledge about the university. By administering assignments related to exploring the requirements for attending that particular university, the student would have an opportunity to engage in academic tasks related to her personal dream and aspiration. Additionally, the student could use mathematical concepts to determine how much money would need to be saved to pay for the first year of tuition, room and board, and potential books. Since the student is passionate about attending that school, the student will be more motivated to complete assignments related to it. This same approach can be employed for students who dream of playing professional sports, owning a business, entering the medical profession, or any other post-secondary endeavor. If students share their dreams, the educator can connect them to academic content in ways that affirm students and challenge them academically.

Strategies for Leveraging Dreams to Promote Literacy Skills

While I could provide a plethora of strategies across different disciplines, I chose to focus solely on literacy for brevity's sake. Additionally, I focused on literacy because, as a nation, we have consistently struggled to maximize student performance concerning literacy. To assist in this endeavor, I suggest integrating students' dreams and aspirations with literacy instruction. In the K–12 setting, educators can employ various writing assignments to encourage young people to dream while cultivating literacy skills. Here are a few:

1. **Personal Narrative Prompts**
   a. *Assignment*:
      i. Provide students with an opportunity to write about their dreams and aspirations.
         1. *Possible Questions to Spur Writing*:
            a. What college or university would you choose to attend if you received a full scholarship? Provide at least three details to support your decision.
            b. If you were a successful business owner who could afford to buy anything you desired, what would you purchase first and why? Please elaborate.
            c. If you could visit any country, which place would you go to? Please explain.

2. **Future Self Prompt**
    a. *Assignment*:
        i. Allow students to write a letter to their future self, ten years from now. Ask students to describe what their future selves are doing now and what they have accomplished over the last ten years.
            1. *Possible Questions*:
                a. What was your grade point average (GPA) when your future self graduated high school? What did your future self do to achieve that GPA?
                b. What college or workforce experiences did your future self find the most fascinating? What lessons have you learned along your journey?
                c. What adversities or challenges did your future self have to overcome to become successful? How did you do it?
3. **Collaborative Writing**
    a. *Assignment*:
        i. Provide students with an opportunity to work with a partner or group to draft a motivational speech to be delivered to a large group of elementary students.
            1. *Potential Titles or Prompts*:
                a. "Dream Big"
                b. "Never Give Up"
                c. "Attitudes for Success"

The writing assignments mentioned above can enhance students' creative and critical thinking skills while also allowing them to share their perspectives and aspirations beyond the classroom context. Writing assignments that inspire aspirational thinking can help provide young people with guidance and direction as they seek to navigate toward a future they desire for themselves. After educators read and review students' work, educators will possess intimate details about each student's intentions for their future. Affirming students about their dreams and providing feedback to help students achieve their dreams are the critical next steps for educators. This can be a gamechanger for educators who desire to create student-centered, culturally responsive, and aligned instruction.

Reflective Questions for Chapter 4

What are your dreams as an educator? What are your dreams concerning the students you teach? How can educators incorporate students' dreams in the academic space to inspire learning? How can students' dreams be leveraged to connect with students on a deeper level? How might students' dreams be used as tools to develop student-centered, culturally responsive, and aligned instruction? Martin Luther King Jr. is a prime example of how powerful dreams can be. In his case, he used a dream to forecast a picture of a more perfect union. He described a union as "indivisible with liberty and justice for all." His dream became a rallying cry, not just for a marginalized community but for an entire nation. This is the power of dreams. How many students have dreams in their hearts that may lead to transformational change in their communities and the world? We will never know if we are unwilling to center students' dreams in the academic space.

In this chapter, we discussed the personal connection between a student's dreams, their future aspirations, and the effort they put forth in the academic space. I have contended that a student will be more motivated to learn in school when they see how their dreams and future aspirations are connected to the academic content. In order for teachers to connect a student's dreams and aspirations to the academic content, the teacher must first learn about their students' dreams and aspirations. This is the prerequisite to integrating dreams and aspirations into the learning environment. While teachers can use a few strategies mentioned in Chapter 1 (student interest surveys, questionnaires, one-on-one interviews), this chapter encourages teachers to use strategic writing assignments that provide students with opportunities to explore their dreams and future aspirations through literacy. Leveraging students' dreams to promote literacy instruction can be a powerful strategy for strengthening students' writing skills while centering students' interest in the classroom.

Review of Summarized Findings from This Chapter:

1. Every student has dreams, defined as *strong desires, goals, or aspirations they wish to accomplish.*
2. Dreams, as aspirations, help to reveal what a person values and deems meaningful and worthy of pursuit.
3. Knowledge of students' dreams can be leveraged to build relationships with students and their families.
4. Knowledge of students' dreams can also be leveraged to introduce academic content and help students make connections between their ambitions and the skills they need to develop in school.
5. Educators can and should use literacy instruction to foster students' dreams.
6. Writing assignments can be administered to center students' dreams and cultivate creative and critical thinking skills.

References

Emdin, C. (2022). *Stem, steam, make, dream: Reimagining the culture of science, technology, engineering, and mathematics*. International Center for Leadership in Education from Houghton Mifflin Harcourt Publishing.

Hart, C. S. (2016). How do aspirations matter? *Journal of Human Development and Capabilities*, *17*(3), 324–341. Routledge.

Section 2
How Do I Teach?

Guiding Question #2: How Do I Teach?

In the first section, we focused on the guiding question, "Who Do I Teach?" The purpose of Section 1 was to ensure that educators prioritize compassion before content. Some would say, "Reach before you teach" or "Maslow before you Bloom," but no matter what we call it, the goal is always to remain student-centered in everything we do. For that reason, the first four chapters highlighted a need to gather pertinent demographic information about the students we serve so we can teach with students in mind at all times.

In Chapter 1, we explored the need to center student *Identity* and get to know them on a personal level. By centering students' personal and social identities, educators can establish a positive rapport with students and ultimately reduce the number of students who feel "anonymous" in schools. In Chapter 2, we discussed the need to center students' *Culture*. By leveraging students' cultural backgrounds, lived experiences, preferences, and interests, teachers will be in the best possible position to employ culturally responsive instructional practices to motivate and engage an increasingly diverse student population.

In Chapter 3, we introduced the concept of *Empowerment* to emphasize the need to cultivate student efficacy. As we know, not all students are intrinsically motivated to succeed academically when entering schools. Therefore, it is important for teachers to utilize strategies to empower young people in the academic setting. Lastly, we concluded Section 1 by discussing the need to center students' *Dreams*. Dreams and aspirations are powerful tools that can motivate students. Additionally, students' dreams and aspirations reveal what students value. When educators attempt to gain knowledge about students' identities, cultural backgrounds, empowerment needs, and dreams, educators can truly say they are student-centered.

In the next section, we move on from "Who Do I Teach" to "How Do I Teach?" This requires us to place a strategic focus on instructional methodology. Now that we know who we teach, the most important question becomes how we teach them. Let's dive in!

5

The "T" in I.C.E.D. T.E.A.

Transformative Rapport

Rapport vs Relationships

During my 17 years of experience working in the K–12 education setting, I have heard countless educators equate relationships to rapport. In fact, many educators believe the two words are synonyms. This is not true. In this chapter, I argue that while these concepts are related, they are not identical. According to the Cambridge Dictionary, "relationship" is "the way in which things are connected or work together." Yet, "rapport" is defined as "a good understanding of someone and an ability to communicate well with them." Based on these technical definitions, having a relationship with someone implies that two people are connected, whereas rapport with a person describes the type of connection that has been established.

If we analyze the technical dictionary definitions, we may agree that one can be connected to someone whom one does not have a good understanding of. Similarly, one can work with someone while not communicating well with them. This means that it is possible to be in a relationship with someone while lacking a positive rapport with them. In the context of education, this manifests daily. Unfortunately, for far too many teachers and

DOI: 10.4324/9781003613626-7

students, they work together and are connected but they may not understand each other or communicate well with one another.

Rapport Is a Deeper Connection

I argue that rapport is much deeper than relationships because it often describes the relationship. It is similar to a thermometer in the sense that it provides us with a reading of the relationship. Is it a positive relationship, or is it a negative relationship? Is it a shallow relationship, or is it a deep relationship? Rapport will let us know. For example, I have to engage the cashier whenever I go to the grocery store. I have to exchange my money for items I intend to purchase. Therefore, the cashier and I have a relationship simply because we have to work together and connect to some degree. However, our connection may be shallow. It may not have any depth to it. I may not know if the cashier has children, pets, or family in another state. I may not know the cashier's last name, favorite food, or weekend hobbies. Furthermore, the cashier may not know any details about me. So, we have a relationship, but it is transactional at best. We are connected but we lack rapport.

To be honest, many teacher-student relationships resemble the relationship I mentioned between myself and the cashier at the grocery store. It is transactional at best. The student enters the class, the teacher provides the instruction, and the student regurgitates what they have learned. It's a simple transaction or exchange of information. Instead of money being exchanged for groceries, the student exchanges time for academic knowledge. This type of interaction or transaction will not significantly alter the trajectory of a student's life. These shallow encounters will not inspire a student to become the best version of himself or herself. Rapport is what leads to life transformation and academic success.

Rapport and Student Success

In her book *Culturally Responsive Teaching and the Brain*, Zaretta Hammond (2015) explains that rapport is connected to the idea of trust and affirmation within a relationship. Hammond argues that rapport begins with empathy and "listening with grace"

(p. 78). Cornelius-White (2007) conducted a meta-analysis and found that strong rapport within teacher-student relationships, characterized by empathy, warmth, and encouragement, significantly enhances student achievement. Other researchers, like Roorda et al. (2011), have found that helping students feel valued and supported leads to better academic outcomes. These findings have been corroborated for years by new teachers as well as veterans.

One veteran educator, Rita Pierson, prioritized building rapport with students for 40 years. She shared some of her experiences as a teacher in a now viral TED Talks Education video released in 2013. In that video, Pierson explained how one of her teacher colleagues approached her and said, "They don't pay me to like the kids. They pay me to teach a lesson. The kids should learn it. I should teach it, they should learn it. Case closed!" Basically, this teacher colleague expected the teacher-student relationship to be transactional. She did not expect to invest in the rapport-building process with her students. Yet, Rita Pierson provided that teacher with invaluable advice. She said, "Kids can't learn from teachers they don't like." In other words, establishing positive rapport with students is critical to academic success.

Deepening Our Understanding of Rapport

Researchers Linda Tickle-Degnen and Robert Rosenthal (1990) explain that rapport is expressed best when people say they "clicked" with someone or have good "chemistry" (p. 286). According to Tickle-Degnen and Rosenthal, three essential components are present when a high degree of rapport is experienced: 1) mutual attentiveness, 2) positivity, and 3) coordination.

Component #1 – Mutual Attentiveness

"Mutual attentiveness" occurs when two people mutually express interest in what the other says and does (p. 286). In education, mutual attentiveness may look like a teacher expressing interest in students and students expressing interest in teachers. Teachers may demonstrate mutual attentiveness by attending students' events outside of school (e.g., attending a student-athlete's sporting event, a birthday party, or a dance recital off campus). By attending a student's events off campus, the teacher sends a message communicating to the student that "I care about what you care about." Likewise, a student may demonstrate mutual attentiveness by inquiring about a teacher's life outside of work (e.g., asking questions about a teacher's plans for the weekend, expressing interests about a teacher's family life, etc.). Tickle-Degnen and Rosenthal argue that mutual attentiveness is the first essential component that creates focused and cohesive interactions that "form the structure of rapport" (p. 286).

Component #2 – Positivity

The second component is the presence of "positivity" during interactions (p. 286). Similar to the first component, the positivity component must be mutually experienced to be considered rapport. In other words, if a teacher interacts with a student and perceives it as positive, it does not necessarily mean the student will agree that the interaction was positive. Positivity occurs when both individuals in the relationship feel friendly and caring toward one another. This has significant implications for educators because many say, "I have a positive relationship with my students." Yet, if students do not echo that same sentiment, the positivity component of rapport may be absent. This component sheds light on the fact that rapport is not a one-way street but rather a mutual and shared experience.

Component #3 – Coordination

The third and final component that evidences high levels of rapport in a relationship is "coordination" (p. 286). When considering coordination, terms such as "balance, harmony, and 'in sync' come to mind" (p. 286). It describes the predictability of behaviors between individuals who have established rapport in their relationship. In other words, individuals who have a rapport with each other understand how one another will respond to certain situations. This is because they have established a chemistry in the relationship that allows them to be in sync with one another on an emotional level. When this occurs, misunderstandings and miscommunications are less likely to happen. In education, teachers who have established rapport with students are able to predict student behaviors based on their knowledge of students. For example, a teacher who works closely with a student will understand what may frustrate or trigger that student. That teacher will be able to de-escalate and defuse potential behavioral issues because of the rapport that has been established. Likewise, a student who has established rapport with a teacher will anticipate that teacher's response to a particular situation because of the rapport established in their relationship. The student who is redirected after getting up out of his seat without permission may say, "I knew you would say that" in response to the teacher's directive to ask for permission. This level of coordination and predictability is a consequence of rapport.

Transformative Rapport Is the Goal

As indicated by the work of Tickle-Degnen and Rosenthal, rapport is distinguished from relationships. Rapport goes further in that it describes the chemistry and harmony within the relationship. Additionally, rapport involves mutual feelings, perceptions, and behaviors regarding the relationship. For teachers who desire to positively impact students' academic and behavioral performance, establishing a positive rapport is essential. Hopefully, this chapter has shown why striving to develop relationships with students is good but not good enough. This is because not all relationships are mutually perceived as positive. The goal for educators should be to create a positive rapport so impactful that it changes the course of a young person's life for the better. Maya Angelou has a great quote that speaks to the heart of rapport. She stated, "People will forget what you said, people will forget what you did, but people will never forget how you made them feel." That's the power of rapport. Remember that rapport manifests as mutual attentiveness, positivity, and coordination. Each teacher must strive to establish a positive rapport with students that inspires them to believe in their inherent brilliance while empowering them to reveal it to the world.

Transformative Rapport Defined

Transformative rapport refers to a deep, positive connection that is validating, affirming, and life changing. This is the type of rapport that alters the trajectory of a person's life for the better. It influences individuals to develop a mindset committed to becoming the best versions of themselves. For students, this results in a commitment to lifelong learning. For educators, it looks like an unwavering commitment to one's purpose in this work of teaching and learning. When teachers strive to establish transformative rapport with students, they seek to build trust, mutual respect, and understanding. This type of rapport fosters a supportive learning environment for students and educators. From a teacher's perspective, transformative rapport equips the educator with an ability to respond effectively to students' individual needs and challenges. Hammond (2015) refers to this concept as "cognitive insight" (p. 75). According to Hammond, cognitive insight "is about making the invisible visible so the teacher is able to get a better understanding of the student's thinking routines" (p.75). The goal for the teacher is to leverage rapport to meet students' needs and ultimately inspire them to reach their potential in and out of school.

> Transformative rapport refers to a deep, positive connection that is validating, affirming, and life changing.

Transformative rapport helps students feel valued and understood, inspiring them to take greater ownership of their education and personal development. When educators make transformative rapport the goal and intentionally invest time in ensuring it is being established, educators will have the best chance of changing the trajectory of a child's life for the better. This is the ultimate goal of great teachers.

A Personal Story of Transformative Rapport

In 2012, I was working as a high school special education teacher. I had a customized caseload that was tailor-made for me. It consisted of about 17 predominantly Black boys, all of whom had been identified under the IDEA category of emotional disability.

Generally speaking, my students were brilliant but boisterous. They had tremendous potential, but their inability to discipline themselves often hindered their academic progress. I knew my effectiveness in terms of helping my students succeed would be centered around changing their beliefs about school, educators, and – most importantly – themselves. Therefore, I knew I had to establish a positive rapport with each of them.

This was not easy, mainly because many of my students came from single-parent homes that lacked a strong male presence. All of my students had to adjust to being corrected and held accountable by a male figure. Initially, this was difficult for many of them. In addition, many of my students had experiences with the criminal justice system and the foster care system. They had learned to accept the fact that adults would betray their trust. These realities made establishing rapport extremely challenging for me. Nevertheless, I was committed to the process. Each day, I attempted to draw my students one step closer to me as a person. I shared my personal experiences as a young man growing up in a single-parent home. I shared personal stories about my life as a failing high school student who skipped 16 days of school during my freshman year. In addition, I shared how a few teachers refused to give up on me even though I often wanted to give up on myself. I wanted to create a common bond by inviting my students into my world through my personal stories. I also allowed them to invite me into their world through journal entries that required them to reveal a greater level of vulnerability.

Over time, I believe a positive rapport and a caring classroom culture were established. This was evidenced by my students' academic and behavioral progress. While all of my students made great strides, one student stood out more than most; his name was Rudy. Rudy was placed on my caseload during his freshman year and would remain until he graduated. He had been found eligible for special education services during his elementary years as a student with a developmental delay (DD). As he graduated to middle school, he aged out of DD and was found eligible for services as a student with a specific learning disability (SLD). By the time he reached my caseload, he had been serviced in the emotional disability setting and the SLD setting. Although he had been receiving special education services for most of his K–12 experience, I always knew Rudy was highly intelligent. I told him on a regularly basis and often addressed him as "young scholar."

When Rudy became a senior, I told him he would run his Individualized Education Program (IEP) meetings. I also encouraged him to take more advanced courses, which he did. I was very intentional about connecting with him on a personal level and leveraging that connection to challenge him academically. Rudy ended up graduating high school with honors. Ironically, his senior year was also my last year at that school. That year, I won teacher of the year and overall city-wide teacher of the year for my school district. After that, I was presented with an opportunity to take on a new role as a Title 1 Instructional Coach at a middle school. After about two years of serving as the Title 1 Instructional Coach, I received a phone call from the school secretary. She explained that a reporter was on hold and desired to speak to me about one of my former students. I honestly did not know what to expect.

She passed the reporter through to my office phone. The reporter explained that she was preparing to release a story about a former student of mine who had attended the local community college and graduated in just two years. She said the student's name was Rudy. As soon as she said his name, I was immediately overwhelmed with joy because I knew Rudy had overcome the odds. Of all students with disabilities, students identified as having an emotional disability have the highest rates of dropping out of high school (Sparks, 2014). In addition, a recent study exploring the link between disability and incarceration highlighted the fact that "sixty-six percent of incarcerated people self-reported a disability" (Bixby et al., 2022). Hearing of Rudy's successes filled me with satisfaction, fulfillment, and hope as an educator. I knew we had accomplished something amazing. Not only did we prove that students with disabilities can achieve a high level of academic success, but we also successfully disrupted the school-to-prison pipeline that disproportionately impacts Black males with disabilities.

During my conversation with the reporter, she explained that Rudy had mentioned my name as a catalyst for his success. After she shared some of the pertinent details with me about Rudy's perspective of my impact on his life, it was as if someone started chopping onions in my office. Tears of joy started to stream down my face. Sensing that I was overwhelmed with emotion, the reporter said, "I will send you a copy of the article on the day it is released."

When I received my copy of the article, I read each word with a sense of satisfaction, fulfillment, and purpose. Yet, of the entire article, one sentence stood out more than the others. The sentence read, "Mr. Taylor saw something in me and encouraged me to go to college." My eyes were fixated on the four words that read "saw something in me." It made me realize that cultivating rapport with students sometimes requires educators to "see them" and "see something" in them. Educators must see the potential and purpose in every child. Educators must see the brilliance, gifts, and talents that might be overshadowed by student behavior. Educators must see a brighter future for young people, encourage them to go after it, and support them throughout the process. By doing this, educators can change the trajectory of students' lives. This is what I mean when I describe transformative rapport.

Strategies for Establishing Transformative Rapport With Students

Although Rudy said I profoundly impacted his life, I will be the first to say that the sentiment is mutual. Remember that rapport is not a one-way street; it is a mutual experience. Rudy profoundly changed my pedagogy and ignited a passion within me to help young people actualize their potential. I've been on that same mission since Rudy was my student.

Here are a few strategies that I used to establish transformative rapport throughout my career as an educator:

- ♦ **Strategy #1 – "2 × 10 Chat"**
  - **Two minutes per day:** The teacher dedicates two minutes each day to a casual, one-on-one conversation with a specific student. This conversation should focus on topics unrelated to school or academic work, such as the student's interests, hobbies, family, or any other topics that the student finds enjoyable.

- **Ten consecutive days:** This two-minute interaction is repeated for ten consecutive school days. Consistency is the key to building trust and demonstrating genuine interest in the student's life.
  - ☐ **Goal** – This strategy aims to create a positive connection and show the student that the teacher cares about them as a person, not just as a student.

◆ **Strategy #2 – Sharing Personal Stories**
- As this chapter indicates, rapport is best understood as mutual understanding. The goal must be to move beyond transactional relationships. It is insufficient for teachers to know everything about the students, while the students know very little about the teachers. Share your personal stories with your students! This can be done by journaling with students when writing assignments are administered. In addition, this can be done casually at the beginning of class or during the close of a lesson.
  - ☐ **Goal** – The goal of this strategy is to model the same vulnerability that is expected from students.

◆ **Strategy #3 – Active Listening**
- Active listening requires educators to be in tune with their verbal and nonverbal communication cues. This means ensuring that their body language communicates attention and empathy when students share their perspectives. This can be done by paying close attention to what students are saying and then responding thoughtfully.
  - ☐ **Goal** – The goal is to ensure students feel their voices are heard and valued.

Reflective Questions for Chapter 5

What is the difference between relationship building and rapport building? What can you do to demonstrate to yourself that you are committed to the rapport-building process? If you explained the distinction between relationships and rapport to your students, would your students say you have been committed to the rapport-building process? Would your students be more likely to describe their relationship with you as shallow or deep, positive or negative? Would your students be more likely to describe the relationship you have established with them as transactional or life-changing? What are your favorite strategies or activities for developing positive rapport with your students? Can you recall any success stories with your students that resulted from your investment in the rapport-building process?

In this chapter, we distinguished relationships from rapport. While both are essential to the teaching and learning process, this chapter contends that rapport is much more of a thermometer for relationships because it provides a reading or measure of the warmth contained in a relationship. Remember that rapport is defined as "a good understanding of someone and an ability to communicate well with them." This is what must take place in schools between teachers and students. Both parties must develop a good understanding for one another. In addition, both parties must develop an ability to communicate well with one another. If this does not occur, teaching and learning at a high level will never happen. With that being said, establishing transformative rapport between teachers and students is paramount.

> **Review of Summarized Findings from This Chapter:**
> 1. Understand that rapport and relationships are related but not synonyms.
> 2. Remember that just because you have a relationship with someone, it does not mean you have established a positive rapport with them.
> 3. Rapport is "a good understanding of someone and an ability to communicate well with them."
> 4. Building rapport with students requires intentionality on behalf of educators.
> 5. The three essential components of rapport are: 1) mutual attentiveness, 2) positivity, and 3) coordination.
> 6. Establishing positive rapport with students is powerful enough to alter the trajectory of their lives for the better.
> 7. Transformative rapport refers to a deep, positive connection that is validating, affirming, and life-changing.

References

Bixby, L., Bevan, S., & Boen, C. (2022). The link between disability, incarceration, and social exclusion. *Health Affairs, 41*(10). https://doi.org/10.1377/hlthaff.2022.00495

Cornelius-White, J. (2007). Learner-centered teacher-student relationships are effective: A meta-analysis. *Review of Educational Research, 77*(1), 113–143.

Hammond, Z. L. (2015). *Culturally responsive teaching and the brain: Promoting authentic engagement and rigor among culturally and linguistically diverse students*. Corwin.

Roorda, D. L., Koomen, H. M. Y., Spilt, J. L., & Oort, F. J. (2011). The influence of affective teacher-student relationships on students' school engagement and achievement: A meta-analytic approach. *Review of Educational Research, 81*(4), 493–529.

Sparks, S. (2014, November 26). Emotionally disturbed students at greatest risk of dropping out, study finds. *EducationWeek*. https://www.edweek.org/teaching-learning/emotionally-disturbed-students-at-greatest-risk-of-dropping-out-study-finds/2014/11

Tickle-Degnen, L. & Rosenthal, R. (1990). The nature of rapport and its nonverbal correlates. *Psychological Inquiry, 1*(4), 285–293.

6

The "E" in I.C.E.D. T.E.A.
Engaging Instruction

The Necessity of Engagement

For decades, researchers (e.g., Fredricks et al., 2004) have elevated engagement as the antidote to poor outcomes regarding student achievement in schools. From "low levels of academic achievement, high levels of student boredom and disaffection, and high dropout rates in urban areas," engagement is often cited as the most powerful variable associated with student outcomes (p. 59). Yet, there is not a consensus on how student engagement should be defined. Some researchers believe "engagement is located within students" (Hazel et al., 2013) and others believe engagement is a school construct (Fredricks et al., 2004).

Over the last 20 years, numerous definitions for "engagement" have emerged in educational research literature. Bomia et al. (1997) refer to student engagement as a "student's willingness, need, desire and compulsion to participate in, and be successful in, the learning process" (p. 294). Daggett (2005) defines student engagement as "the degree to which students are motivated and committed to learning, demonstrate positive behaviors and attitudes, and have relationships with adults, peers, and parents that support learning" (p. 38). Fletcher (2015) explained, "Students are engaged when they are attracted to their work, persist despite challenges and obstacles, and take visible delight in accomplishing their work" (p. 1).

For the purposes of establishing a general definition for this book, I argue that student engagement in school is defined as "the extent to which students' demonstrate their commitment to the learning process." While I do believe a student's commitment to the learning process will vary based on a multitude of factors (e.g., emotional maturity, situational challenges, physical fatigue, academic stamina), I believe teachers have an enormous influence on whether or not a student chooses to engage in the learning process. For example, Johnny (a pseudonym) might be an engaged student during science class but a disengaged student during English class. Johnny's disengagement from English might not be due to factors outside of the school context but rather solely related to how the English teacher delivers instruction and engages him in the learning process. For this reason, this chapter focuses on the necessity of engaging instruction. Educators must understand that engagement is nuanced and must be viewed through the lens of behavioral engagement, emotional engagement, and cognitive engagement. Therefore, I believe engaging instruction meets the needs of students and maximizes their commitment to learning across the behavioral, emotional, and cognitive dimensions.

> Engaging instruction meets the needs of students and maximizes their commitment to learning across the behavioral, emotional, and cognitive dimensions.

Three Dimensions of Engagement

Although some educators attempt to simplify engagement, it is a multifaceted and complex construct. Fredricks et al. (2004) conceptualize three dimensions of engagement: Behavioral engagement, emotional engagement, and cognitive engagement. Let's look into these dimensions.

1. **Behavioral Engagement**
    a. According to Fredricks et al. (2004), behavioral engagement "draws on the idea of participation; it includes involvement in academic and social or extracurricular activities and is considered crucial for achieving positive academic outcomes and preventing dropping out"

(p. 60). This definition goes beyond how students participate during a teaching lesson. It also takes into consideration how students interact broadly within the school context. Are students disengaged during direct and explicit instruction? Are students disengaged during recess, student assemblies, or other events and activities hosted by the school? This component is a holistic measure of student behavior engagement as it relates to the school setting. It also sheds light on issues pertaining to student discipline. How are teachers constructing lessons and delivering instruction that satisfy the behavioral dimension of engagement?

2. **Emotional Engagement**
    a. The emotional engagement component encompasses all aspects of students' emotionality. According to Fredricks et al. (2004), "Emotional engagement refers to students' affective reactions in the classroom, including interest, boredom, happiness, sadness, and anxiety" (p. 63). This definition has many implications for educators. We must consider how students respond to their teachers, classmates, instruction, and the school on an emotional level. Do students feel a sense of belonging and acceptance when they enter the classroom? Do students feel cheerful and excited when engaged in direct and explicit instruction? How do the curriculum materials and instructional delivery within the academic setting influence students on an emotional level? It is important for educators to consider how the school or classroom setting contributes to adolescent moodiness and the potential for behavioral concerns. This component influences whether a student chooses to engage or disengage from the learning process. It is important to note that emotional engagement is profoundly related to rapport.

3. **Cognitive Engagement**
    a. Fredricks et al. (2004) state, "cognitive engagement draws on the idea of investment; it incorporates thoughtfulness and willingness to exert the effort

necessary to comprehend complex ideas and master difficult skills" (p. 60). This component is heavily connected to measures of student achievement. Student achievement is often measured by formal and informal assessments administered to evaluate what students have learned (we will cover this in greater detail in Chapter 7). Through the lens of cognitive engagement, students' willingness to demonstrate their achievement requires their desire to exert the effort necessary to comprehend complex ideas and master difficult skills. While in the ideal world all students would enter the classroom motivated to learn, we know this is not the case for all students. Therefore, teachers must empower students (for more about empowering students, revisit the strategies in Chapter 3). A reflective question for educators to ask themselves is this: Are we engaging students with rigorous, cognitively demanding work that challenges them to think critically? If not, why not? What can we do differently to engage students in the dimension of cognitive engagement.

Strategies for Designing Instruction With the Three Dimensions of Engagement in Mind
Behavioral Engagement
The dimension of behavioral engagement draws on the idea of participation. The reflective question educators must ask themselves is, how can I increase student participation and engagement during the teaching and learning process? It has been well documented that increasing the use of technology, hands-on, project-based learning, and the integration of music can bolster student participation in the learning environment.

- **Technology**
  - Teachers can utilize tools such as smartboards, educational apps, and online quizzes to make lessons more interactive and dynamic for student consumption. Technology can facilitate real-time feedback, visual demonstrations, and interactive activities that

capture students' attention and cater to different learning styles. In addition, technology is a culturally responsive instructional tool for a generation of students who are self-proclaimed "gamers."

♦ **Hands-On, Project-Based Learning**
  • Teachers can use manipulatives, experiments, and group projects to provide students with practical, real-world experiences. Hands-on activities help students actively engage with the material, reinforce learning through practice, and make abstract concepts more concrete and understandable. In addition, grouping students or arranging teams can help cultivate students' social awareness while increasing participation. Many students enjoy socializing with their age-group peers. Moreover, students who are usually considered to be "talkative" can thrive when project-based and group assignments are employed. This is because these assignments provide space and opportunity for talking in class. Therefore, employing project-based learning and group assignments can help teachers to better manage behaviors and meet the unique needs of students. Lastly, hands-on, project-based learning is an effective strategy to yield 100% engagement in a classroom.

♦ **Music and Movement**
  • Music has a plethora of applications within the K–12 classroom. Teachers can use music during classroom transitions or to establish classroom routines. This application allows music to be a tool to provide students with direction. It can also be incorporated into the class to offer students a "brain break" (a brief pause to relax) after a rigorous assignment. This application of music can be a tool to support the emotional wellness of students. Additionally, it can be used as an instructional tool to teach scientific concepts such as sound waves. Science teachers are likely to increase students' interest in science by employing their favorite songs in the classroom setting to engage students in an experiment that

requires them to measure sound waves. English and language arts teachers can use music as a supplemental aid during writing assignments. Secondary English teachers could use songs to teach a lesson on poetry or figurative language. In some cases, teachers may simply use music as background noise to create a specific tone or atmosphere within the classroom. Nevertheless, integrating music into the academic setting can help to increase students' behavioral engagement.

Emotional Engagement

The dimension of emotional engagement draws on student emotionality. While I definitely suggest that teachers adjust their instructional delivery by teaching with greater passion and enthusiasm, teachers must think holistically about emotional engagement. The reflective question educators must ask themselves is, how can I create an emotionally healthy and safe learning environment for each student in my class? How can I ensure that each child feels emotionally secure enough to learn? While there is a plethora of strategies that teachers can use to design lessons that increase emotional engagement, I encourage educators to start with intentionally creating an atmosphere that centers the ICED principles mentioned in the first section of this book: *Identity, Culture, Empowerment,* and *Dreams*. If a teacher can create a classroom culture where all students have learned to value one another's identities, cultural backgrounds, empowerment needs, and dreams, I would argue that social and emotional success has been achieved in that space. Let's review how we might be able to employ the I.C.E.D. principles to achieve social emotional success for students:

- ♦ **Center Identity**
  - Centering students' identities will foster a sense of belonging and acceptance that is necessary to help each student feel emotionally safe in the learning environment. In addition, centering students' identity may look like ensuring students see their identities reflected and valued in the classroom and within the instructional

materials. This can boost students' confidence, self-esteem, and engagement. Research tells us that students are more likely to engage deeply with instructional material when it connects to their own experiences and identities, leading to more meaningful learning outcomes (Ladson-Billings, 1994; Hammond, 2015; Gay, 2018; Taylor, 2022). In addition to "get-to-know-you" activities, teachers can center students' identities by administering projects and group assignments that require students to collaborate to create group auto-biographies. Students can work as a team to identify commonalities and differences among members of the group they have been assigned to. By administering a simple rubric, teachers can instruct students to identify areas of commonality and differences within the group (e.g., foods, hobbies, musical interests).

♦ **Center Culture**
- Centering students' cultural backgrounds can help to increase students' skills in cultural competence, which are essential for navigating an increasingly diverse world. Additionally, exposing students to diverse cultures within the classroom broadens students' perspectives and fosters a more inclusive worldview. This can enhance their critical thinking and citizenship skills while promoting mutual respect and understanding among diverse students. If educators desire to contribute to a world that overcomes xenophobia, cultural biases, and stereotypes, centering culture may be helpful. Teachers can center students' culture by using culturally inclusive instructional materials and resources.

♦ **Center Empowerment**
- Teachers can center the principle of empowerment in the classroom by hanging motivational posters or implementing classroom core values that use language associated with empowerment and encouragement. Another strategy for empowering students involves the intentional use of academic praise. Academic praise

occurs when a "teacher gives a verbal or nonverbal statement or gesture to provide feedback for appropriate academic performance" (Dudek et al., 2018, p. 293). Academic praise has been proven to increase student engagement. In addition to the use of encouraging communication and the employment of academic praise, teachers are encouraged to design and deliver instruction in a way that inspires students to take ownership of their learning. This means providing a level of independence that fosters a sense of agency. Students need to be explicitly empowered to develop persistence in the academic space as well as outside of the school context. Another practical strategy for empowering students is to utilize one-on-one meetings and personalized notes to foster empowerment.

- **Center Dreams**
  - Teachers can center students' dreams by providing students with time and space to explore, brainstorm, and create a vision for themselves as successful in the future. As students begin to think about their dreams and aspirations, they will gain an understanding of the post-secondary endeavors they want to pursue after they graduate from high school. In addition, teachers can use goal-setting assignments to teach students about S.M.A.R.T. goals (specific, measurable, attainable, realistic, and time-based). Activities that require students to create smart goals will prepare them to embrace the process that leads to goal attainment. Encouraging students to dream big can empower and motivate them in the academic space and beyond.

Cognitive Engagement

The dimension of cognitive engagement draws on students' willingness to exert the mental effort necessary to comprehend complex ideas and master difficult skills. In other words, teachers must be able to lead students in cognitively challenging and enriching work. The reflective question educators must ask themselves is, how can I build students' confidence to engage in a rigorous curriculum? According to Ainsworth and Donovan (2019), the purpose of a rigorous curriculum is "to raise the level of teaching and learning so that students are prepared for the future with skills that drive knowledge economies: innovation, creativity, teamwork, problem solving, flexibility, adaptability, and a commitment to continuous learning" (p. xxiii). First, teachers must be able to design assignments that spur a high level of critical and creative thought. Then, teachers must be able to teach in a way that builds confidence and efficacy within each student so they are willing to engage with the material that will ultimately challenge them cognitively and intellectually. I will address issues surrounding cognitive engagement, rigorous curriculum, and the need for alignment more thoroughly in the next chapter. For now, here are five strategies that can help teachers increase students' cognitive engagement:

1. **Scaffolded Guided Practice:** Offer support and feedback during practice sessions until students can perform tasks independently.
2. **Graphic Organizers:** Use charts, diagrams, and other visual aids to help students structure and synthesize information.
3. **Socratic Seminar or Socratic Questioning Strategy:** Ask open-ended questions that promote discussion and require students to justify their answers with evidence.
4. **Project-Based Learning:** Design projects that connect academic content to real-world issues or career paths.
5. **Hands-On Activities:** Incorporate experiments, role-plays, or projects that require students to physically engage with the content.

Reflective Questions for Chapter 6

Why is engagement necessary? What is the relationship between student achievement and student engagement? How would you describe "engagement" in your own words? What might be the challenges or barriers that interfere with student engagement in your classroom or school community? From your perspective, what does an engaged classroom look like? What are some of your favorite strategies for increasing student engagement in your classroom? What are your thoughts on the three dimensions of engagement discussed in this chapter? How might you plan instruction to increase behavioral engagement? What strategies might you use to increase students' emotional engagement? In what ways can increasing students' cognitive engagement impact student outcomes?

In this chapter, we covered the necessity of student engagement. In an ideal world, every student would enter classrooms fully motivated and inspired to learn academic concepts. Yet, we do not live in an ideal world. Thus, educators must be persistent in their attempts to engage students in the teaching and learning process. As mentioned in this chapter, engagement has different dimensions. Students must be engaged behaviorally, emotionally, and cognitively. To accomplish this task, educators are encouraged to employ the principles discussed in Chapters 1–4. This will allow educators to develop the type of rapport that provides insight into what students find engaging. Teachers must always remember that what works for one student may not necessarily work for all students. Therefore, teachers should be prepared to commit to the ongoing process of learning how students prefer to engage in the teaching and learning process. Additionally, teachers must be reflective and willing to adjust their methods over time.

> **Review of Summarized Findings from This Chapter:**
> 1. Many researchers have linked student disengagement to poor student academic outcomes.
> 2. There is not an agreed-upon definition of engagement in educational research literature.
> 3. Engaging instruction meets the needs of students and maximizes their commitment to learning across the behavioral, emotional, and cognitive dimensions.
> 4. Integrating technology, hands-on/project-based learning opportunities, and music into the classroom can increase students' behavioral engagement.
> 5. Centering students' identities, cultures, needs for empowerment, and dreams can help students develop emotional engagement.
> 6. Utilizing scaffolds, graphic organizers, and open-ended questioning techniques can foster critical and creative thinking while increasing students' cognitive engagement.

References

Ainsworth, L. & Donovan, K. (2019). *Rigorous curriculum design: How to create curricular units of study that align standards, instruction, and assessment.* International Center for Leadership in Education from Houghton Mifflin Harcourt.

Bomia, L. et al. (1997). The impact of teaching strategies on intrinsic motivation. *Opinion Papers*, 1–28. https://eric.ed.gov/?id=ED418925

Daggett, W. (2005). High school reinvention. In *High School Reinvention Symposium*. Washington, DC.

Dudek, C. M., Reddy, L. A., & Lekwa, A. J. (2018). Measuring teacher practices to inform student achievement: A predictive validity study. *Contemporary School Psychology, 0*, 1–11. doi:10.1007/s40688-018-0196-8

Fletcher, A. (2015, March 29). Defining student engagement: A literature review. *SoundOut*. https://adamfletcher.net/2015/03/29/defining-student-engagement-a-literature-review/

Fredricks, J. A., Blumenfeld, P. C., & Paris, A. H. (2004). School engagement: Potential of the concept, state of the evidence. *Review of Educational Research, 74*(1), 59–109. https://doi.org/10.3102/00346543074001059

Gay, G. (2018). *Culturally responsive teaching: Theory, research, and practice* (3rd ed.). Teachers College Press.

Hammond, Z. L. (2015). *Culturally responsive teaching and the brain: Promoting authentic engagement and rigor among culturally and linguistically diverse students.* Corwin.

Hazel, C. E., Vazirabadi, G. E., & Gallagher, J. (2013). Measuring aspirations, belonging, and productivity in secondary students: Validation of the student engagement measure. *Psychology in the Schools, 50*(7), 689–704. doi:10.1002/pits21703

Ladson-Billings, G. (1994). *The dreamkeepers: Successful teachers of African American children.* Jossey-Bass.

Taylor, J. H. (2022). Relationship between multicultural consciousness and culturally responsive teaching self-efficacy (Order No. 30241427). Available from *ProQuest Dissertations & Theses Global*. (2753378936). https://go.openathens.net/redirector/liberty.edu?url=https://www.proquest.com/dissertations-theses/relationship-between-multicultural-consciousness/docview/2753378936/se-2

7

The "A" in I.C.E.D. T.E.A.
Aligned Curriculum

A Common Story: "Kids Can't Shine When Instruction Is Not Aligned"

Mary, a middle school science teacher, is passionate about space exploration and astrophysical research. This particular passion is the reason why she desired to become a science teacher in the first place. While she understands that in her district the curriculum explicitly states that students are required to develop an understanding of planetary objects, specifically moons, stars, asteroids, and comets, she occasionally goes off track during her lessons to expose students to a new phenomenon discovered in the 1960s known as pulsars and quasars. So, instead of spending adequate time teaching students about planets, moons, stars, asteroids, and comets (what is contained in the written curriculum), Mary spends too much time covering pulsars and quasars, which are concepts that are not found in the curriculum.

Then, when it came time to administer the district-wide science benchmark tests, Mary noticed that most of her students performed poorly on the planetary objects unit. Mary, unaware of the fact that she failed to properly align the curriculum and instruction within her classroom, developed a false perception of her students' academic potential. So, she walked into her grade-level professional learning community (PLC) meeting and lamented that she had been given a group of "low-performers." Mary is basing her perception of her students' capabilities on the results from the benchmark. Still, she is failing to take into consideration that her instruction was not in alignment with the curriculum.

This type of scenario occurs far too frequently in schools across the United States. In some cases, the lack of student achievement and the widening academic achievement gaps across our nation are largely due to teachers failing to align curriculum, instruction, and assessments. That's why teachers need to develop an understanding of what students are required to learn first; then, they must seek to understand the best way to effectively deliver student-centered, culturally responsive, and aligned instruction.

Curriculum Alignment

According to Cornell University's Center for Teaching Innovation, curriculum alignment is the process of aligning the written curriculum, the teaching methodologies that will be used, and the assessments that will be employed to evaluate learning. Depending on your geographical context, educators may use phrases such as "aligning the curriculum, instruction, and assessments (CIA)" or "aligning the written, taught, and assessed," but they are referring to the same concept. Curriculum alignment may seem like a singular or simple concept, but I argue that it is a multistep process that requires higher-level thinking, analytical capabilities, and creative thinking skills. This is because in order to align curriculum, instruction, and assessments, teachers must identify the learning outcomes (what must be taught), the best instructional strategy to ensure learning is occurring (delivery of instruction), and the methods for measuring if learning is occurring (assessments). In order to effectively execute this process, teachers must receive explicit training and professional development.

> Curriculum alignment is the process of aligning the written curriculum, the teaching methodologies that will be used, and the assessments that will be employed to evaluate learning.

Training Educators for Curriculum Alignment

In my opinion, educators cannot have a conversation about equipping teachers to align the curriculum without mentioning the work of Larry Ainsworth. Larry Ainsworth is an educator and consultant who has made significant contributions to the field of education through his focus on improving teaching practices and ensuring that curriculum and instruction align with educational standards. Two of his books that have been my "go-to reads" for aligning curriculum are *Unwrapping the Standards: A Simple Process to Make Standards Manageable* and *Rigorous Curriculum: How to Create Curricular Units of Study That Align Standards, Instruction, and Assessment* (2nd ed.), which he co-authored with Kyra Donovan. Both of these books are tremendous resources that educators need in their repertoire if the goal is aligning curriculum, instruction, and assessments to maximize student achievement. Based on the work of Larry Ainsworth, here is a simple, step-by-step process that can help educators align the curriculum.

Step 1 – Understand the Priority Standards

Ainsworth and Donovan (2019) believe educators must align curriculum, instruction, and assessments and provide students with rigorous and relevant learning opportunities that are designed to raise students' critical thinking skills. For Ainsworth and Donovan, the first thing educators must do is "prioritize the standards" (p. 1). In other words, teachers must understand the "priority standards." Priority standards are defined as "a carefully selected subset of the total list of the grade-specific and course-specific standards within each content area that students must know and be able to do by the end of each school year in order to be prepared for the standards in the next grade level or course" (p. 9). Each grade level and each subject has priority standards that are usually established by the state department of education. These standards identify the skills students must be able to perform and the concepts that students must learn. "Priority Standards are the focal point in the design of a rigorous and relevant curriculum" (Ainsworth & Donovan, 2019, p. 97). Therefore, educators need to understand the priority standards first.

Step 2 – Unwrap the Standards

Once educators are aware of the priority standards, they need to learn how to unwrap them. Unwrapping the standards refers to "analyzing and deconstructing the wording of grade-level and course-specific Priority Standards within each unit of study to determine exactly what students need to know (teachable concepts) and be able to do (specific skills)" (Ainsworth & Donovan, 2019, p. 97). When analyzing the standards, Ainsworth and Donovan (2003) encourage educators to circle the verbs and underline the nouns. He offers this simple strategy because the nouns represent the teachable ideas or concepts students must know, and the verbs represent the specific skills students must be able to perform.

By unwrapping the standards, educators will be better equipped to answer the following questions:

1. What content must be taught?
2. What are the learning intentions, targets, and outcomes?
3. What do my students need to know by the end of this unit or year?
4. How should I teach my students so they will develop the skills and master the concepts?
5. What strategies are most appropriate to help me teach the skills and concepts required by the standards?
6. How rigorous should my instruction be based on the cognitive demand required by the standards?

Step 3 – Determine the Rigor

While many educators often define "rigor" as "more challenging work," Ainsworth and Donovan (2019) define rigor as "a quality of instruction that requires students to construct meaning for themselves, impose structure on information, integrate individual skills into processes, operate within but at the outer edge of their abilities, and apply what they learn in more than one context and to unpredictable situations" (p. 101). In other words, rigor should be associated with "complexity" and not "difficulty" alone. Increasing the rigor of assignments should mean challenging students to apply critical thinking and higher-order thinking skills. Rigor challenges students to solve complex problems. Once teachers effectively unwrap the standards, they will know how rigorous the instruction and the assessments need to be to match the rigor implied in the standards. Ainsworth offers three tools to help teachers determine the appropriate levels of rigor: 1) Bloom's Taxonomy, 2) Webb's Depth of Knowledge, and 3) Hess' Cognitive Rigor Matrix. Teachers can use these resources to ensure their instruction aligns with the curriculum.

Step 4 – Identify the Big Idea

Ainsworth and Donovan also encourage educators to identify the "Big Ideas" or foundational understandings and key principles that they want their students to learn prior to the end of a particular unit of study. The "big ideas" are also known as "lightbulb moments" (p. 109). These are the moments of realization and discovery that indicate student learning has occurred and students are able to prove their understanding. When teachers develop an understanding of the big ideas, they will be better equipped to guide students during instruction so students can also discover the big ideas of a particular lesson or unit.

Step 5 – Establish Essential Questions

According to Ainsworth and Donovan (2019), essential questions are "engaging, open-ended questions that educators use to spark student interest in learning the content of the unit about to commence" (p. 117). Essential questions should be rooted in the standards, and they should correspond to the big ideas. At the end of the lesson or unit, each student should be able to respond to the essential questions to demonstrate their understanding. Ultimately, these questions guide teachers' lesson planning and instructional delivery. They are designed to ensure that each student has made progress toward the overall learning goals and intentions associated with the particular standards that must be taught. Therefore, establishing essential questions that are aligned to the priority standards is a necessary component of high-quality teaching and learning. Teachers can post these questions in the front of the classroom, preferably next to the date and learning objective for ease of visibility. Teachers can sequentially follow these five steps to ensure their instruction is effectively aligned with the written curriculum. (For additional support aligning curriculum, instruction, and assessments, please see the Appendices at the back of the book.)

But ... What Exactly Is a "Curriculum"?

We have already established the importance of aligning the curriculum, instruction, and assessments, but let's take a moment to zoom in on the concept of curriculum. What exactly are we talking about when we say "curriculum"? David A. Squires is an Associate Professor of Educational Leadership at Southern Connecticut State University and the author of *Aligning and Balancing the Standards-Based Curriculum*. In his book, Squires (2005) explains that:

> A curriculum is the plan that focuses and guides classroom instruction and assessments. Usually, curriculum refers to the organized framework that guides what is and should be taught in schools. For example, if a social studies curriculum specifies a unit on World War I, teachers need to instruct on World War I and not the Great Depression or current events.
>
> (p. 4)

Curriculum Determines Teaching Priorities

While increasing students' knowledge of the Great Depression and other current events is important and valuable, the curriculum ultimately determines teaching priorities. Even if a teacher believes students should know about the Great Depression in the third grade, the teacher is not solely responsible for what should be included in the third-grade curriculum. From that standpoint, teacher autonomy is somewhat limited by the curriculum. The limits imposed on educators by the curriculum have been debated since the 1950s. For example, renowned African American scholar of multicultural education, James A. Banks, has strongly advocated for a multicultural curriculum instead of what he referred to as a "mainstream-centric curriculum" (p. 151). According to Banks (2016), the dominant curriculum in K–12 schools, colleges, and universities is a mainstream-centric curriculum that primarily reflects the experiences of mainstream Americans. Banks explained, "A curriculum that focuses on the experiences of mainstream Americans and largely ignores the experiences, cultures, and histories of other ethnic, racial, cultural, language, and religious groups have negative consequences for both mainstream students and students of color" (p. 152). For this reason, curriculum reform has been a highly debated topic in education.

Although many scholars and practitioners agree that a multicultural curriculum would be most beneficial, few will argue that curriculum across the United States is multicultural. Nevertheless, if educators want to improve the current levels of student achievement, they must continue to align their instruction and assessments with the current curriculum as written. This is because students will be assessed based on what is contained in the current curriculum. When teachers introduce concepts not contained in the curriculum, students can become experts in areas that will not be measured on assessments. While gaining knowledge is usually beneficial in the context of school, the curriculum ultimately determines what knowledge will be evaluated. If a student becomes an expert in an area that he or she will never be assessed on, we will never know that the student is an expert in that area. This is because assessments used to measure student achievement in K–12 schools are designed to measure knowledge that aligns with the written curriculum. It is also noteworthy to mention that a low score on a state-sanctioned assessment based on the state-mandated curriculum does not necessarily indicate a lack of intelligence, but rather is an indication that the particular student fails to demonstrate proficiency in relation to knowledge and skills associated with the state-mandated curriculum.

Student-Centered and Culturally Responsive Curriculum?

One might wonder, "If the dominant curriculum is mainstream-centric, how can teachers make the written curriculum student-centered and culturally responsive?" This is an important question. To make any curriculum student-centered and culturally responsive, educators have two options: 1) Change the curriculum entirely, or 2) change the way the curriculum is taught. Undoubtedly, changing the curriculum would be the fastest way to ensure students have access to materials that are student-centered and culturally responsive. However, this process is much more complicated, presents more obstacles, and is more time-consuming when compared to changing one's instructional delivery. Also, the ability to change a curriculum is usually above a teacher's pay grade. Typically, it is the responsibility of school-district curriculum writers, school boards, and state education departments. As I stated earlier, curriculum reform has been and continues to be a highly debated topic in education.

Direct Instruction Based on the Curriculum

While most teachers may not be in a position to change the curriculum, they can easily change how it is presented to students (instruction). The curriculum determines what must be taught but not necessarily how it must be taught. This is why the design and delivery of instruction are of the utmost importance to educators who want to improve student achievement through a student-centered, culturally responsive, and aligned methodological approach. Teachers have some creative freedom to deliver direct instruction based on the curriculum provided. Direct instruction is "a type of explicit teaching that is performed directly by a teacher to their students" (Engelmann, 2024, p. 21). The goal of direct instruction is to accelerate student learning and performance. As it pertains to engaging diverse students in direct and explicit instruction based on the curriculum, teachers must possess the pedagogical dispositions and technical skills required to effectively deliver instruction that results in learning. In addition, teachers must be able to integrate insights gained about students' identities, cultural backgrounds, empowerment needs, and dreams. This will ensure that the lesson is engaging for students. Banks (1989) highlights a few approaches educators can employ to center diverse students' identities and cultures during instruction.

Four Approaches to Teaching Curricula With Diverse Students in Mind

Contributions Approach

The first approach is "the contributions approach" (p. 17). Banks explains, "The contributions approach is the easiest approach for teachers to use to integrate the curriculum with ethnic content." Teachers can simply integrate heroes and holidays that are significant in various cultures to personalize student learning. While this approach can help to expose students to individuals and special days that are significant across different cultures, it has serious limitations. According to Banks, "The contributions approach often results in the trivialization of ethnic cultures, the study of their strange and exotic characteristics, and the reinforcement of stereotypes and misconceptions" (p. 17). This is most likely because the contributions approach does not help students develop a global and historical view of issues related to the heroes and holidays being integrated into the curriculum. If a teacher intends to use a contributions approach, it is essential to help students understand the historical context around the heroes and holidays being integrated into the curriculum. By helping students understand the historical context in which the cultural contributions (heroes and holidays) are positioned, teachers can elevate rigor and empower students to develop analytical and critical thinking skills.

Additive Approach

The second approach discussed by James Banks is "The additive approach" (p. 17). Like the contributions approach, the additive approach does not change the structure, purposes, and characteristics of the current curriculum. It simply allows teachers to add content to the existing curriculum. Similar to the contributions approach, the additive approach has serious limitations and drawbacks. The major issue with this approach is based on who will select the content (concepts, events, issues, and topics) desired to be added to the curriculum. If one teacher is solely responsible for determining which elements should be added to the lesson design, students will likely receive a lesson that fails to help students develop multiple perspectives about global and historical issues. For example, if a teacher adds a guided practice activity featuring Martin Luther King Jr.'s famous "I Have a Dream" speech to an English lesson, the teacher can ultimately shape students' understanding of the author's purpose. What if the teacher is not aware of the historical context of that speech? What if the teacher is uncomfortable discussing topics such as racism, oppression, and the marginalization of people of color? If the teacher lacks cultural competence and historical awareness, the teacher may be likely to teach Martin Luther King Jr.'s speech while evading the broader discourse about historical racism, oppression, and the marginalization of people of color. If this discourse is evaded, students will develop a misunderstanding of Dr. King's speech. For reasons such as this, the additive approach presents just as many problems as the contributions approach.

Transformation Approach

The third approach is "The transformation approach" (p. 18). This approach is fundamentally different from the contributions and additive approach because it "enables students to view concepts, issues, themes, and problems from several perspectives and points of view"; whereas the contributions and additive approaches center the perspective of mainstream Americans without offering perspectives of individuals from diverse cultural groups. For example, the Virginia Department of Education outlines specific standards or learning targets for the geometry curriculum. One standard states, "The student will determine the relationships between the measures of angles and lengths of sides in triangles, including problems in context" (Virginia Department of Education, 2018. Using this standard, a mathematics teacher could align instruction with the curriculum by teaching students how to determine the relationships between measures of angles and lengths of sides in the Great Pyramid in Egypt. By doing this, the teacher would be demonstrating the contributions and additive approach because the curriculum would remain unchanged, but students would have gained insight about the use of mathematics, angles, and measurements by diverse cultures to build pyramids in Egypt.

Using the same geometry curriculum and example of the geometry standards, a teacher could employ the transformation approach by utilizing question techniques to prompt students to think about how various cultures around the world used geometric insight, knowledge, and skills to construct large triangular monuments. The teacher could place students in teams to complete a project-based assignment that requires them to identify triangular architectural designs constructed and erected across the world. Using factual information about the size and scope of the designs, students could determine the relationships between the measures of angles and lengths of sides in the triangular architectural designs. As an exit ticket, the teacher could prompt students to discuss how different cultures applied mathematical and geometrical concepts to measure angles in their societies. This type of assignment would be aligned with the learning targets and expectations of the Virginia geometry curriculum, and it would help students consider the viewpoints and perspectives of people from different cultures who have used geometry to create triangular architectural structures around the world. This is one example of how to align curriculum and employ a transformational approach that enables students to view concepts, issues, and themes from several perspectives and points of view.

Social Action Approach
The fourth and final approach listed by James Banks is the "social action approach" (p. 161). According to Banks (1989), "The social action approach includes all elements of the transformation approach but adds components that require students to make decisions and take actions related to the concept, issue, or problem studied in the unit" (p. 161). The major instructional goals related to this approach include teaching students critical thinking and decision-making skills. Banks believes students should possess the ability to "become reflective social critics and skilled participants in social change" (p. 161). Therefore, teachers who use the social action approach must always elevate rigor, challenge students to think critically, and help students develop self-advocacy skills that will allow them to one day become active participants in social change.

Considering the social action approach, Banks (1989) states, "teachers are agents of social change who promote democratic values and the empowerment of students" (p. 162). The social action approach requires students to demonstrate learning by solving problems and addressing issues. Teachers can utilize this approach in a variety of ways through project-based and group assignments focused on responding to critical issues within society. Each of the four approaches can be used simultaneously while aligning the current curriculum. The next question we must ask ourselves is, how do we assess whether students are learning from our aligned, rigorous, and relevant curriculum?

What Are Assessments?

Once teachers successfully engage students in student-centered, culturally responsive, and aligned instruction, they must assess or measure student learning. To better understand this process, educators must develop an understanding for what an assessment is. Over the course of my career, my understanding of the significance of assessments has been heavily influenced by the insight and work of Dr. Robert Marzano. In his book titled *Classroom Assessment and Grading That Work* (2006), Robert Marzano explains that an assessment is any "planned or serendipitous activities that provide information about students' understanding and skill in a specific measurement topic" (p. 35). Marzano is a strong believer in the power of assessments. He stated that the classroom assessment "might be one of the most powerful weapons in a teacher's arsenal" (p. 2). Marzano believes this because for the past 50 years effective classroom assessments have been proven to improve student achievement (Bloom, 1978; Lysakowski & Walberg, 1981; Kumar, 1991; Black & William, 1998; Hattie, 1999; Haas, 2005; Marzano, 2010).

When discussing concepts related to assessments, educators often mention formative and summative assessments. Marzano differentiates the two by highlighting the fact that a formative assessment is an ongoing assessment that can be administered at any point while knowledge is being learned, meaning that a teacher can employ a formative assessment at any point during the teaching and learning process to ensure students are grasping concepts. These assessments are usually ongoing and more frequent when compared to summative assessments because the information gained from formative assessments allows teachers to modify their approach to teaching and learning to ensure all students are learning. However, summative assessments are only administered "at the end of a learning episode" (Marzano, 2006, p. 8). Once a teacher administers a summative assessment, it usually signifies the conclusion or end of a unit or course. For that reason, summative assessments are also referred to as end-of-course assessments. The implication is, modifying and adjusting instruction is highly unlikely once a summative assessment is administered. For these reasons, formative assessments are more useful to teachers and they "produce the more powerful effect on student learning" (Marzano, 2006, p. 9).

How to Effectively Use Formative Assessments

As already mentioned, formative assessments are defined as "any activity that provides sound feedback on student learning" (Marzano, 2006, p. 11). These assessments are most useful to teachers because they provide them with insight about student learning that allows teachers to adjust and modify their instructional approach to the benefit of students. Additionally, these assessments allow teachers to provide students with specific feedback that allows students to improve upon their performance on future assignments. Marzano emphasizes that the feedback given by teachers based on formative assessments should do two things: First, feedback "should give students a clear picture of their progress on learning goals and how they might improve," and secondly, feedback should encourage students to improve (p. 6). Marzano believes teachers must provide feedback in a way that motivates students to make an effort to achieve at a higher level. The implication is teacher feedback can have a positive or negative impact on students. This is why teachers must prioritize relationships and develop positive rapport with students. If teachers are not careful with how they communicate with some students, the feedback they provide can discourage student learning and achievement. As we discussed in Chapter 3, teachers must always strive to empower students.

Summary: Five-Step Process for Centering Students and Aligning the Curriculum, Instruction, and Assessments

The following five-step process can help educators keep students at the center of the teaching and learning process:

- **Step 1:** Prioritize rapport to develop an understanding of your students' interests, needs, and preferences.
- **Step 2:** Develop an understanding of what students must know based on the written curriculum (Larry Ainsworth calls it "unwrapping the standard").
- **Step 3:** Brainstorm creative ways to integrate students' lived experiences, interests, needs, and preferences into a lesson plan design (apply culturally responsive teaching practices).
- **Step 4:** Design the aligned lesson that centers your students' identities, cultures, empowerment needs, and dreams.
- **Step 5:** Deliver engaging instruction, assess student learning, and reflect on ways to improve your practice while empowering students to achieve at a higher level.

Reflective Questions for Chapter 7

Why should every teacher learn how to align the curriculum? What can happen if a teacher aligns instruction with the curriculum but fails to align the assessments with the instruction? How are student outcomes influenced when teachers fail to align the curriculum, instruction, and assessments? What does it mean to "unwrap" the standards? What will happen to student outcomes if teachers provide less rigorous instruction than the standards demand? How might students respond if teachers teach the curriculum without considering students' interests, needs, and preferences? How can feedback provided to students impact their desire to put forth effort in the academic setting? How should an educator respond to a "mainstream-centric curriculum" that fails to include and honor racially and culturally diverse groups of people?

This chapter focused on the necessity of aligning curriculum, instruction, and assessments to ensure that students are effectively engaged in the teaching and learning process. Teachers must possess five technical skills associated with providing students with access to quality instruction. These skills include: 1) "unwrapping" or analyzing the curriculum to determine what students need to know and be able to do based on the curriculum, 2) identifying "big ideas" from the standards that we want students to gain from our instruction, 3) communicating those ideas to students in student-friendly language, 4) creating essential questions to be used during direct and explicit instruction, and 5) employing a culturally responsive instructional delivery to ensure high quality instruction engages and meets the diverse needs of all students.

Review of Summarized Findings from This Chapter:

1. Curriculum refers to the organized framework that guides what is and should be taught in schools.
2. Curriculum alignment is the process of aligning the written curriculum, the teaching methodologies that will be used, and the assessments that will be employed to evaluate learning.
3. Teachers must be coached and trained to understand and "unwrap" the priority standards outlined in the curriculum.
4. Teachers must also learn how to determine the rigor demanded by the standards in order to teach students with the appropriate level of cognitive demand.
5. Teachers must be willing to use a multicultural and culturally responsive instructional approach because curricula may exclude or misrepresent artifacts and examples of culturally and racially diverse groups.
6. Assessing students can have a positive impact on student achievement.

References

Ainsworth, L. (2003). *Unwrapping the standards: A simple process to make standards manageable.* Lead + Learn Press.

Ainsworth, L. & Donovan, K. (2019). *Rigorous curriculum design: How to create curricular units of study that align standards, instruction, and assessment.* International Center for Leadership in Education from Houghton Mifflin Harcourt.

Banks, J. A. (1989). Approaches to multicultural curriculum reform. *Trotter Review*, 3(3), 17–19. https://scholarworks.umb.edu/trotter_review/vol3/iss3/5

Banks, J. A. (2016). Approaches to multicultural curriculum reform. Eds. Banks, J. A & Banks, C. A. M., *Multicultural education: Issues and perspectives* (9th ed.). Wiley.

Black, P. & William, D. (1998). Assessment and classroom learning. *Assessment in Education*, 5(1), 7–75.

Bloom, B. S. (1976). *Human characteristics and school learning.* McGraw-Hill.

Engelmann, K. (2024). *Direct instruction: A practitioner's handbook.* John Catt Educational.

Haas, M. (2005). Teaching methods for secondary algebra: A meta-analysis of findings. *NASSP Bulletin*, 89(642), 24–46.

Hattie, J. (1999, August). Influences on student learning (Inaugural professorial address, University of Auckland, New Zealand). https://www.researchgate.net/publication/237248564_Influences_on_Student_Learning

Hattie, J. (2009). *Visible learning: A synthesis of 800+ meta-analyses on achievement.* Routledge.

Hattie, J. (2016). Third Visible Learning Annual Conference: Mindframes and Maximizers, Washington, DC, July 11.

Hattie, J. & Timperley, H. (2007). The power of feedback. *Review of Educational Research*, 77(1), 81–112.

Kumar, D. D. (1991). A meta-analysis of the relationship between science instruction and student engagement. *Education Review*, 43(1), 49–66.

Lysakowski, R. S. & Walberg, H. J. (1981). Classroom reinforcement in relation to learning: A quantitative analysis. *Journal of Educational Research*, 75, 69–77.

Marzano, R. J. (2006). *Classroom assessment and grading that work*. Association for Supervision and Curriculum Development.

Marzano, R. J. (2010). *Formative assessment & standards-based grading*. Marzano Research.

Squires, D. (2005). *Aligning and balancing the standards-based curriculum*. Corwin.

Virginia Department of Education. (2018). Science standards of learning for Virginia public schools. https://www.doe.virginia.gov/teaching-learning-assessment/k-12-standards-instruction/science/standards-of-learning

Conclusion: Fill Your Cup First

Now that we have explored the I.C.E.D. T.E.A. Framework, you are better equipped to center your students' identities, cultural backgrounds, empowerment needs, and dreams. Remember that this is the prerequisite for designing student-centered, culturally responsive, and aligned instruction. As stated earlier, the best instructional strategy a teacher can possess is knowledge of the students they teach. Therefore, seeking to establish transformational rapport must become a top priority. Learning about our students will allow us to integrate aspects of their lived experiences into the instructional design. The goal is to design effective lessons that the students enjoy and desire to engage in, not lessons that teachers enjoy and desire to teach. This work is not about us; it's about the students we serve. To fully grasp this understanding, we need a fundamental mindset shift from the teacher-centered pedagogy that seems to dominate the field of education to a student-centered pedagogy that elevates students' interests, preferences, and needs. While this book is designed to equip teachers with a new mindset, teachers cannot do this work without school leaders.

The Critical Role of School Leaders – Principal Power

School leaders are critical to the implementation of a student-centered pedagogy. The reality is that teachers do not have the power and authority to cast a compelling instructional vision for a school. Teachers barely have the power to create a vision for the classrooms they lead. They usually are responsible for implementing the instructional vision that is handed down by the school principal. From that standpoint, principals are usually the most powerful individuals within the school context. They chart the instructional course, establish the pedagogical expectations, and determine what the professional development priorities will be.

With that being said, imagine what would happen to the student-centered and culturally responsive teacher who works for a principal who is more standards-driven than student-driven. Imagine the anxiety that might spring forth in a teacher trying to personalize learning in an environment that is compliance-driven but not culturally responsive? How can teachers thrive if they are not adequately supported and empowered to do what is best for the diverse students within their classroom context? Teachers need support.

"Teachers Cannot Pour From an Empty Cup"

Decades of educational research validate the effectiveness of many high-yield strategies on student achievement. However, no strategy or variable comes close to the impact a teacher can make on student learning. A plethora of researchers have suggested that teachers are the single most influential school-related factor to student achievement (Aaronson et al., 2007; Cawelti, 1999; Chetty et al., 2014; Darling-Hammond, 2000; Hanushek, 2011; Hattie, 2016; Rivkin et al., 2005; Rockoff, 2004; Stronge & Tucker, 2000). Therefore, the need to support, coach, and retain effective teachers has never been greater. This work is critical because teachers cannot pour from an empty cup.

Capacity Building – Filling Up the Teacher's Cup

If the educational system, including teacher preparation programs, school districts, and building-level leaders, fails to provide effective professional development to bolster teacher capacity, the negative consequences on student achievement will be predictable. Students can only go as far as teachers can take them when it comes to instruction and academic achievement. Therefore, prioritizing the teacher capacity building process should be a central focus of the educational system moving forward.

The reality is that teachers cannot pour from an empty cup. Figuratively speaking, imagine if teachers are provided with a teacup full of iced tea to pour into students' cups. They may be able to pour an ounce of iced tea into one or two students' cups. However, if teachers are supplied with a two-liter bottle of iced tea, they may be able to fill about eight students' cups. If we supply a few gallons of iced tea, they may be able to sufficiently pour enough cups to quench the thirst of every student in their class. The moral of the message is: Capacity determines what teachers can provide to their students. Teachers simply cannot pour what they do not have. The problem is that we are asking teachers to fill students' cups without first ensuring that teachers have the capacity to effectively execute the task we are giving them. Whether you possess a teacup, a two-liter bottle, or a few gallons, your capacity will ultimately determine your limitations. We must commit to filling teachers' cups first.

Hopefully, this book becomes a resource that pours into teachers' capacity. Throughout this book, I have argued that we need a blended instructional approach, one that combines a student-centered, culturally responsive, and aligned instructional methodology that will maximize the teaching and learning process to increase student achievement in the K–12 setting. I have emphasized that students must be centered first. Prior to delivering instruction, teachers need to know and be aware of their students' identities, cultural backgrounds, empowerment needs, and dreams. These components need special consideration during the lesson planning process. Also, I believe instructional materials and the instructional delivery itself must be responsive to the needs, lived experiences, and preferences of diverse students. I have argued that teaching and learning must contain a methodological approach focused on transformational rapport, engaging instruction, and an aligned curriculum. I believe a mindset determined to understand who we teach, and how we ought to teach, can maximize student achievement for all students. We need to employ a blended instructional approach that requires teachers to figuratively pour I.C.E.D. T.E.A.

References

Aaronson, D., Barrow, L., & Sander, W. (2007). Teachers and student achievement in the Chicago public high schools. *Journal of Labor Economics, 25*(1), 95–135.

Cawelti, G. (1999). Improving achievement: Finding research-based practices and programs that boost student achievement. *The American School Board Journal, 186*(7), 34–37.

Chetty, R., Friedman, J. N., & Rockoff, J. E. (2014). Measuring the impacts of teachers I: Evaluating bias in teacher value-added estimates. *American Economic Review, 104*(9), 2593–2632.

Darling-Hammond, L. (2000). Teacher quality and student achievement: A review of state policy evidence. *Education Policy Analysis Archives, 8*(1), 1–44.

Hanushek, E. A. (2011). The economic value of higher teacher quality. *Economics of Education Review, 30*(3), 466–479.

Hattie, J. (2016). Third Visible Learning Annual Conference: Mindframes and Maximizers, Washington, DC, July 11.

Rivkin, S. G., Hanushek, E. A., & Kain, J. F. (2005). Teachers, schools, and academic achievement. *Econometrica, 73*(2), 417–458.

Rockoff, J. E. (2004). The impact of individual teachers on student achievement: Evidence from panel data. *American Economic Review, 94*(2), 247–252.

Stronge, J. H. & Tucker, P. D. (2000). *Teacher evaluation and student achievement*. NEA.

Appendix A: The I.C.E.D. T.E.A. Framework

Concept	Definition	Leveraging Strategy
Identity	In general terms, identity is how you perceive yourself and how you think others perceive you.	Student interest surveys, interviews with students, and interviews with parents
Culture	Culture is the inspiration and chief influence behind all human activity. It impacts how ideas are perceived and how information is processed. It shapes how students make sense of the world.	Cultural competence, empathic disposition, and culturally responsive teaching
Empowerment	To empower students, educators must be willing to intentionally help students increase their belief in their own intellectual power and ability.	Speak life, family engagement, and academic feedback
Dreams	Dreams are strong desires, goals, or future aspirations that a person wishes to accomplish. They may represent what a person intends to achieve or become in life.	Personal narrative prompts, future self prompts, and collaborative writing
Transformative Rapport	Transformative rapport refers to a deep, positive connection that is validating, affirming, and life changing.	2 × 10 chats, sharing personal stories, and active listening

(Continued)

Concept	Definition	Leveraging Strategy
Engaging Instruction	Engaging instruction meets the needs of students and maximizes their commitment to learning across the behavioral, emotional, and cognitive dimensions.	Integrate technology, hands-on, PBL, music and movement, and graphic organizers
Aligned Curriculum	Curriculum alignment is the process of aligning the written curriculum, the teaching methodologies that will be used, and the assessments that will be employed to evaluate learning.	"Unwrap" the priority standards and center students during instructional delivery

© Jahkari H. Taylor

To download the I.C.E.D. T.E.A. Framework, scan the following QR code:

Appendix B: Checklist for Aligning the Curriculum

Larry Ainsworth's process for unwrapping standards is designed to help educators break down and understand educational standards to ensure effective instruction. Here's a checklist that identifies the step-by-step process based on his approach:

Step 1: Identify the Standards

- ♦ **Obtain the Standards:** Start by gathering the relevant educational standards from your curriculum framework or educational authority.
- ♦ **Select the Standard:** Choose a specific standard or set of standards you want to focus on for your lesson or unit.

Step 2: Determine the Learning Goals

- ♦ **Analyze the Standard:** Read the standard carefully (pay attention to key verbs and nouns) to understand its requirements and expectations.
- ♦ **Extract Key Concepts:** Identify the core concepts and skills that the standard addresses.
- ♦ **Define Learning Objectives:** Break down the standard into specific, measurable learning objectives that align with what students need to know and be able to do.

Step 3: Unpack the Standard (Underline the Nouns and Circle the Verbs)

- ♦ **Identify Critical Content:** Determine what essential knowledge and content students need to master. This includes facts, concepts, and principles.

- **Determine Key Skills:** Identify the skills and processes that students need to develop to meet the standard. This might include problem-solving, analysis, or application skills.
- **Establish Depth of Knowledge:** Assess the level of rigor (cognitive complexity) required by the standard, ranging from basic recall to higher-order thinking skills.

Step 4: Design Assessments

- **Create Formative Assessments:** Develop assessments based on the essential questions that correspond with the "big ideas" contained in the standard. Then, employ formative assessments to gauge students' understanding of the content and skills and provide ongoing feedback. These assessments can include quizzes, class discussions, or practice problems.
- **Develop Summative Assessments:** Design end-of-unit or end-of-lesson assessments to measure whether students have met the standard. This can be through tests, projects, or presentations.

Step 5: Plan Instructional Strategies

- **Select Teaching Methods:** Choose instructional strategies and activities that will help students grasp the essential content and skills. This might include direct instruction, collaborative work, hands-on activities, or technology integration.
- **Differentiate Instruction:** Adapt your teaching methods to accommodate different learning styles and needs. Provide various levels of support and challenge to ensure all students can access and engage with the material.

Step 6: Implement the Lesson

- **Deliver Instruction:** Teach the content using the planned strategies and activities. Ensure that instruction is aligned with the unpacked standards and learning objectives.

- **Monitor Progress:** Observe students' understanding and adjust instruction as needed based on their responses and formative assessment data.

Step 7: Reflect and Revise

- **Review Outcomes:** Analyze the results from formative and summative assessments to determine whether students have met the learning objectives.
- **Adjust Plans:** Based on assessment data and student feedback, revise your instructional strategies and plans to address any gaps or areas needing improvement.
- **Reflect on Practice:** Evaluate the effectiveness of your approach and make adjustments to enhance future instruction and student learning.

By following these steps, educators can systematically break down standards into manageable components, design effective instruction, and assess student progress to ensure that all students achieve the desired learning outcomes.

To download the Five Steps to Effective Instruction PDF, scan the following QR code:

Appendix C: CIA Alignment Practice Tool (APT)

Adapted from Ainsworth, L. & Donovan, K. (2019). *Rigorous curriculum design: How to create curricular units of study that align standards, instruction, and assessment.* International Center for Leadership in Education from Houghton Mifflin Harcourt, p. 105)

What is the priority standard?
What are the supporting standards?
Practicing the Unwrapping Process

Concepts (Nouns)	Skills (Verbs)	Rigor (Bloom's)

Next Steps: After Unwrapping the Standard

Essential Questions	
Big Ideas	
Formative Assessments	

To download this tool, scan the following QR code:

Appendix D: The Purpose Pedagogical Approach

PACE Framework
A Reminder for Teachers to "PACE" Themselves

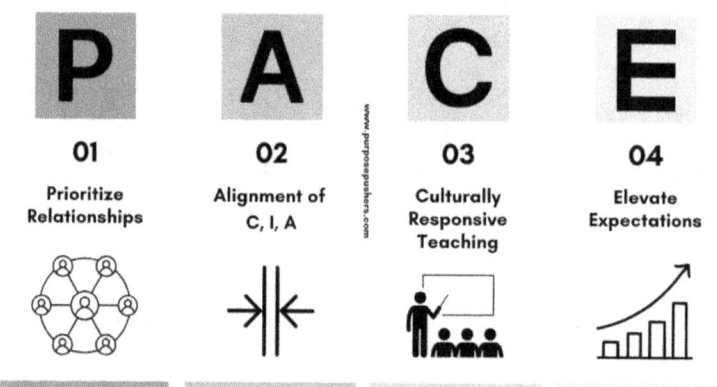

© Jahkari H. Taylor

To download the full-color framework, scan the QR code below:

For Product Safety Concerns and Information please contact our EU
representative GPSR@taylorandfrancis.com
Taylor & Francis Verlag GmbH, Kaufingerstraße 24, 80331 München, Germany

www.ingramcontent.com/pod-product-compliance
Lightning Source LLC
Chambersburg PA
CBHW070403240426
43661CB00056B/2525